G000293516

ROAD ATLAS
IRELAND

8th edition June 2018

© AA Media Limited 2018
Original edition printed 2004

Cartography:
All cartography in this atlas edited, designed and produced by the Mapping Services Department of AA Publishing (A05637).

This atlas contains data available from openstreetmap.org © under the Open Database License found at opendatacommons.org

Publisher's notes:
Published by AA Publishing (a trading name of AA Media Limited, whose registered office is Fanum House, Basing View, Basingstoke, Hampshire RG21 4EA, UK.
Registered number 06112600).
All rights reserved. No part of this publication may be reproduced, stored in a retrieval system, or transmitted in any form or by any means – electronic, mechanical, photocopying, recording or otherwise – unless the permission of the publisher has been given beforehand.

ISBN: 978 0 7495 7988 3

A CIP catalogue record for this book is available from The British Library.

Disclaimer:
The contents of this atlas are believed to be correct at the time of the latest revision. However, the publishers cannot be held responsible or liable for any loss or damage occasioned to any person acting or refraining from action as a result of any use or reliance on any material in this atlas, nor for any errors, omissions or changes in such material. This does not affect your statutory rights. The publishers would welcome information to correct any errors or omissions and to keep this atlas up to date. Please write to the Cartographic Editor, AA Publishing, The Automobile Association, Fanum House, Basing View, Basingstoke, Hampshire RG21 4EA, UK.
E-mail: roadatlasfeedback@theaa.com

Acknowledgements:
AA Publishing would like to thank the following for information used in the creation of this atlas:
Republic of Ireland census 2011 © Central Statistics Office and Northern Ireland census 2011 © NISRA (population data);
Irish Public Sector Data (CC BY 4.0) (Gaeltacht);
logainm.ie (placenames);
Outdoor Recreation NI and Sport Ireland (waymarked trails);
The Wildlife Trust; Global Mapping, Brackley;
Roads Service and Transport Infrastructure Ireland.

Ordnance Survey Ireland open data (boundary data)
Contains public sector information licensed under the Open Government Licence v3.0

Printer:
Wyndeham Peterborough Ltd, UK

Contents

Map pages	inside front cover
Route planning	II–IV
Route planner	II
Travelling by ferry	III
Driving in Ireland	IV
Key to map symbols	1
Road maps 1: 200,000 scale	2–68
Town plans	69–75
Key to town plans	69
Town Plans	70–75
District maps	76–78
Dublin	76–77
Belfast	78
Motorways	79–89
Key to motorway maps	79
Restricted junctions	79
Motorway maps	80–89
Index to place names	90–99
Counties and administrative areas	90
Place name index	91–99
Map pages	100
Distance chart	inside back cover

Scale 1:200,000
3.16 miles to 1 inch
2km to 1cm

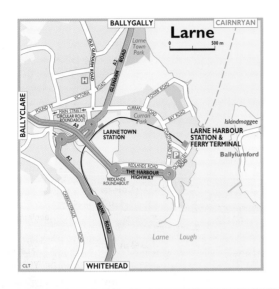

IRISH SEA FERRY CROSSINGS

From	To	Journey time	Operator website
Belfast	Cairnryan	2 hrs 15 mins	stenaline.co.uk
Belfast	Douglas	2 hrs 45 mins (April–Sept)	steam-packet.com
Belfast	Liverpool (Birkenhead)	8 hrs	stenaline.co.uk
Cork (Ringaskiddy)	Roscoff	14 hrs (April–Oct)	brittany-ferries.co.uk
Cork (Ringaskiddy)	Santander	26 hrs (May–Oct)	brittany-ferries.co.uk
Dublin	Cherbourg	18 hrs	irishferries.com
Dublin	Douglas	2 hrs 55 mins (Apr–Sept)	steam-packet.com
Dublin	Holyhead	3 hrs 30 mins	irishferries.com
Dublin	Holyhead	2 hrs	irishferries.com
Dublin	Holyhead	3 hrs 15 mins	stenaline.co.uk
Dublin	Liverpool	8 hrs	poferries.com
Larne	Cairnryan	2 hrs	poferries.com
Rosslare	Cherbourg	18 hrs 30 mins	irishferries.com
Rosslare	Cherbourg	18 hrs 30 mins	stenaline.co.uk
Rosslare	Fishguard	3 hrs 15 mins	stenaline.co.uk
Rosslare	Pembroke	4 hrs	irishferries.com
Rosslare	Roscoff	16 hrs 30 mins (May–Sept)	irishferries.com

Crossings in Ireland

From	To	Journey time	Operator website
Burtonport	Árainn Mhór/Arranmore	15 mins	arranmoreferry.com
Burtonport	Árainn Mhór/Arranmore	15 mins	arranmorefastferry.com
Greencastle	Magilligan	15 mins (Apr–Sept)	loughfoyleferry.com
Passage East	Ballyhack	5 mins	passageferry.ie
Reenard Point	Knightstown (Valentia Island)	5 mins (Apr–Sept)	valentiaisland.ie/getting-here
Strangford	Portaferry	8 mins	nidirect.gov.uk/articles/strangford-ferry-timetable
Tarbert	Killimer	20 mins	shannonferries.com

The information listed is provided as a guide only, as services are liable to change at short notice. Services shown are for vehicle ferries only, operated by conventional ferry unless indicated as a fast ferry service (⛴). Please check sailings before planning your journey.

Roads

Roads in the Republic of Ireland are classified differently to Northern Ireland and the rest of the United Kingdom. Roads are classified as M (motorway), N (national) and R (regional) with road signs reflecting this.

Ireland has improved its road system in recent years, but there are still some poor public roads, especially in rural parts of the country and the further west you travel. Here roads are narrower and patience and care is required.

The road classification in the Republic may give no reliable indication of the width of the road or the surface quality – some main roads are little more than country lanes.

There are no toll roads in Northern Ireland but you'll find tolls on a number of motorways in the Republic of Ireland. Toll roads are shown with a red centre line on the mapping in this atlas. Motorway schematic maps can also be found on pages 79–89.

Speed limits

All public roads have speed limits. Speed limits in the Republic of Ireland are signposted and legislated for in kilometres per hour, whilst in Northern Ireland this is in miles per hour. The two tables below show the national speed limits for each country. National speed limits will apply unless local road signs indicate otherwise.

All drivers must be aware of the speed limit for the road on which they are travelling, and ensure that they drive within the limit for their particular class of vehicle. If the limits are different, the lower of the two will apply.

Road Signs

In the Gaeltacht most road signs are in the Irish language only. In non-Gaeltacht areas signs must appear in both Gaelic and English languages by law. The Irish appears first in italics, with the English underneath.

Northern Ireland road signs are very similar to those in the United Kingdom.

Distances shown on road signs are quoted in miles in Northern Ireland, with kilometres used in the remainder of Ireland. This is reflected on the road maps with miles shown in blue in Northern Ireland, and kilometres in red in the Republic. Speed limit signs also follow this rule.

In order to match the road signs on the ground, the names of places in yellow-shaded Gaeltacht areas are first shown on the maps in this atlas in official Irish. However, to assist those unfamiliar with Irish the English equivalent place name is shown beneath in italics. Both versions of the name appear alphabetically in the index for ease of reference.

In non-Gaeltacht areas the English place name usually appears first, with its Gaelic equivalent beneath.

Northern Ireland - all speed limits in mph

Types of vehicle	Types of road			
	Built up areas*	Single carriageways	Dual carriageways	Motorways
Cars & motorcycles (including car derived vans up to 2 tonnes maximum laden weight)	30	60	70	70
Cars towing caravans or trailers (including car derived vans and motorcycles)	30	50	60	60
Buses, coaches and minibuses (not exceeding 12 metres (39 feet) in overall length)	30	50	60	70
Goods vehicles (not exceeding 7.5 tonnes maximum laden weight)	30	50	60	70†
Goods vehicles (exceeding 7.5 tonnes maximum laden weight)	30	40	50	60

* The 30mph (48km/h) limit usually applies to all traffic on all roads with street lighting unless signs show otherwise.
† 60mph (96km/h) if articulated or towing a trailer.

Republic of Ireland - all speed limits in km/h

Types of vehicle	Types of road			
	Built up areas*	Non-national roads	National roads	Motorways
Cars & motorcycles	50	80	100	120
Cars towing caravans or trailers	50	80	80	80
Single/double-deck buses, coaches for more than 8 passengers (seated)	50	80	80†	100
Single/double-deck buses, coaches (standing passengers)	50	65	65	65
Trucks (gross weight more than 3,500kg)	50	80	80	90

* 30km/h limit applies in special areas near schools and shops where signed
† 100km/h on dual carriageways

The use of speed / safety cameras is employed by both Northern Ireland and the Republic of Ireland as an effective means of automatic speed enforcement.

It is against the law to use a device that can detect or interfere with any speed monitoring equipment when driving in the Republic of Ireland. If you have a sat-nav that shows the location of any fixed speed cameras you must deactivate this function. The Garda (police) will confiscate equipment and can impose on-the-spot fines.

Language

Gaelic (gaeilge) is the official language of the Republic of Ireland although English is very much the every-day, working language.

Gaeltacht is an Irish language term for those areas of Ireland where the Irish language, gaelic, is still spoken as a community language. When passing the road sign **An Ghaeltacht** it means you are entering a Gaeltacht area.

An Ghaeltacht

Gaeltacht areas are shaded yellow on the road maps in this atlas.

Irish road sign found in the Gaeltacht:
Major road ahead – give way to traffic on it

Motoring information

Irish	Symbol	English
Mótarbhealach saor ó dholaí	M1	Toll-free motorway
Mótarbhealach le híoc	M1	Toll motorway
Acomhal lán (1), srianta (2)	(1) (2) (1) (2)	Full (1), restricted junction (2)
Ionad seirbhíse mótarbhealaigh	S Lusk	Motorway service area
Príomhbhealach náisiúnta (IRL)	N17	National primary route (IRL)
Bealach náisiúnta tánaisteach (IRL)	N56	National secondary route (IRL)
Bóthar réigiúnach (IRL)	R182	Regional road (IRL)
Faid i gciliméadar (IRL)	8	Distance in kilometres (IRL)
Príomhbhealach (NI)	A4	Primary route (NI)
Bóthar A (NI)	A21	A road (NI)
Bóthar B (NI)	B75	B road (NI)
Faid i mílte (NI)	5	Distance in miles (NI)
Carrbhealach dúbailte		Dual carriageway
Carrbhealach singil		Single carriageway
Timpeallán		Roundabout
Bóthar á thógáil		Road under construction
Mionbhóthar		Minor road
Droichead nó bóthar le híoc	Toll	Bridge or road toll
Tollán bóthair		Road tunnel
Príomh cheann cúrsa (roghnaithe)	CORK	Primary destination (selected)
Bealach iarainn, stáisiún, crosaire comhréidh, tollán	X	Railway, station, level crossing, tunnel
Páirceáil agus taisteal	P·R	Park and Ride
Créamatóiriam	C	Crematorium
Ospidéal, le hAonad Timpistí & Éigeandála	H H	Hospital, with Accident & Emergency
Teorainn idirnáisiúnta		International boundary
Teorainn eile		Other boundary
Aerfort, aerpháirc		Airport (major/minor)
Carrchaladh	V or	Car ferry
Carrchaladh catamaran		Catamaran car ferry
Farantóireachta paisinéirí	P or	Passenger ferry
Cathair, baile mór, baile beag nó ceantar		City, town, village or locality
Trá, cladach eile		Beach, other foreshore
Airde i méadar	628 ▲	Height in metres

Touring information

Ionad eolais turasóireachta, séasúrach	i i	Tourist information, seasonal
Ionad cuairteoirí nó oidhreachta	V	Visitor or heritage centre
Láithreán campála AA		Camping site (AA inspected)
Mainistir, ardeaglais nó prióireacht		Abbey, cathedral or priory
Ballóg mainistreach, ardeaglais nó prióireacht		Ruined abbey, cathedral or priory
Caisleán, dún		Castle, hill-fort
Gairdín, crannlann		Garden, arboretum
Páirc tuaithe, páirc foraoise		Country park, forest park
Zú, fiabheatha nó páirc éanlaithe, aquarium		Zoo, wildlife or bird park, aquarium
Páirc théama, ionad feirme nó do shláinte ainmhithe		Theme park, Farm or animal centre
Dúlra, tearmann éin	RSPB	Nature, bird reserve
Iontaobhais Caomhnú Fiadhúlra		Wildlife Trust Reserve
Bealach radharcach		Tourist route
Slibhealach le comharthaí	- - -	Waymarked walk
Ionad amhairc, láithreán picnicí		Viewpoint, picnic site
Teach solais, trá		Lighthouse, beach
Ionad siopadóireachta, faichí spóirt nó staidiam		Shopping centre, sports venue or stadium
Galfchúrsa (ar liosta AA)		Golf course (AA listed)
Rásaí capall, ciorcad rásaí cairr		Horse racing, motor-racing circuit
Gníomhaíocht sciála, bádóireacht		Boating, skiing activities
National Trust (NI), An Taisce (IRL)	AT	National Trust site (NI/IRL)
Iarsmalann nó dánlann, Teach nó foirgneamh stairiúil	M	Museum or gallery, Historic house or building
Leacht, leacht réamhstairiúil		Monument, prehistoric monument
Suim tionsclaíoch, uiscrian nó tarbhealach		Industrial interest, aqueduct or viaduct
Láithreán catha le dáta	1690	Battle site with date
Pluais, eas		Cave, waterfall
Muileann gaoithe, drioglann nó grúdlann		Windmill, distillery or brewery
Iarnróid turasóireachta, láthair inspéise eile		Tourist railway, other place of interest
Láithreán Oidhreachta Domhanda (UNESCO)		World Heritage Site (UNESCO)
Léiríonn comharthaí le boscaí tarraingtí laistigh de cheantair uirbeacha		Boxed symbols indicate attractions within urban areas
Ceantair Ghaeltachta		Gaeltacht (Irish language area)
Coillearnach		Woodland

2

239
Bray Head
Bray Head

Ⓐ   Ⓑ   Ⓒ Dromgour

70

Oileán na
gCánóg
Puffin Island

Ⓟ

Ⓓ

Portmagee
An Caladh

395

Ⓥ Skellig
Exper

Sceithigh Riabh.
Knocknaskereightá

R565

Eoilclogh

50

Ring of Kerry
7

Ⓔ

8

Ⓕ

Ⓖ

Loch Món
Lough

Ⓗ amon

1

Bá Fhíonáin
St Finan's Bay

Cill Urlaí
Killurly
331

R566

Baile an Sceilg
Ballinskelligs
Ballinskelligs

R567

Waterville
An Coireán

Loch Luíoch
Lough Currane

An Bh

Loch
Isknag

2

Little Skellig

CEANN DHUICHEALLA
DUCALLA HEAD

410
Bhólais
Bolus

Oileán na gCapall
Horse Island

Bá na Scealg
Ballinskelligs Bay

24

N70

509
Mullach Bóg
Mullaghbeg

Sceilg Mhichil
Skellig Michael

CEANN BHÓLAIS
BOLUS HEAD

Ceann Muice
Hogs Head

499
Cahernageeha
Mountain

Cathair Dónall
Caherdaniel

60

Derrynane Ⓜ
Abbey
Island

Derrynane

3

Scarriff
Island
252

Deenish
Island

Ceann an Uain
Lamb's Head

Kilcathe

Inishfarna

4

C

50

Cod's Head

Eskavaud

Gortaghig

R575

5

Reenroe

BEARA PENINSULA

Dooneen

Allihies
Na hAilichí

Ba

6

Garnish
Bay

Foher

Dursey Island
Cable Car

260

Lackacroghan

Killoug

Cnoc Bólais
252

Dursey Island

Beara Way

Loughnanemore

White Ball
Head

B
H

40

DURSEY
HEAD

Crow
Head

7

8

30

9

10

20

Ⓐ   Ⓑ   Ⓒ   Ⓓ   Ⓔ   Ⓕ   Ⓖ   Ⓗ

'30   40   50

0   1   2   3   4   5 miles
0 1 2 3 4 5 6 7 8 km

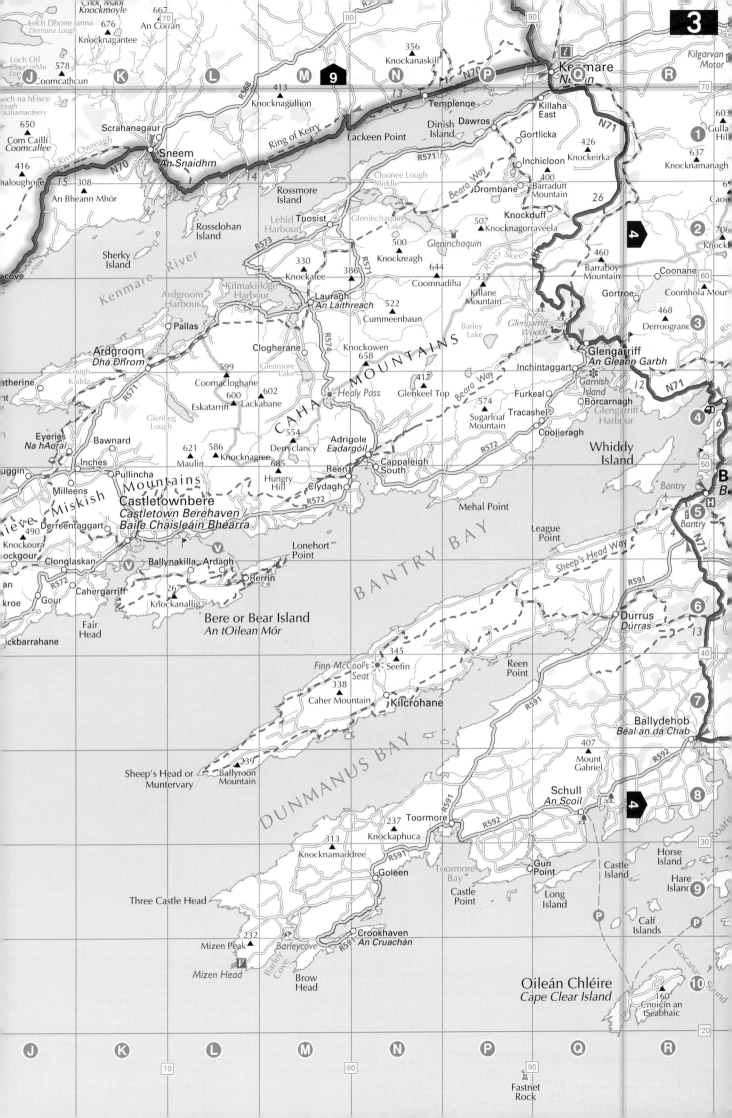

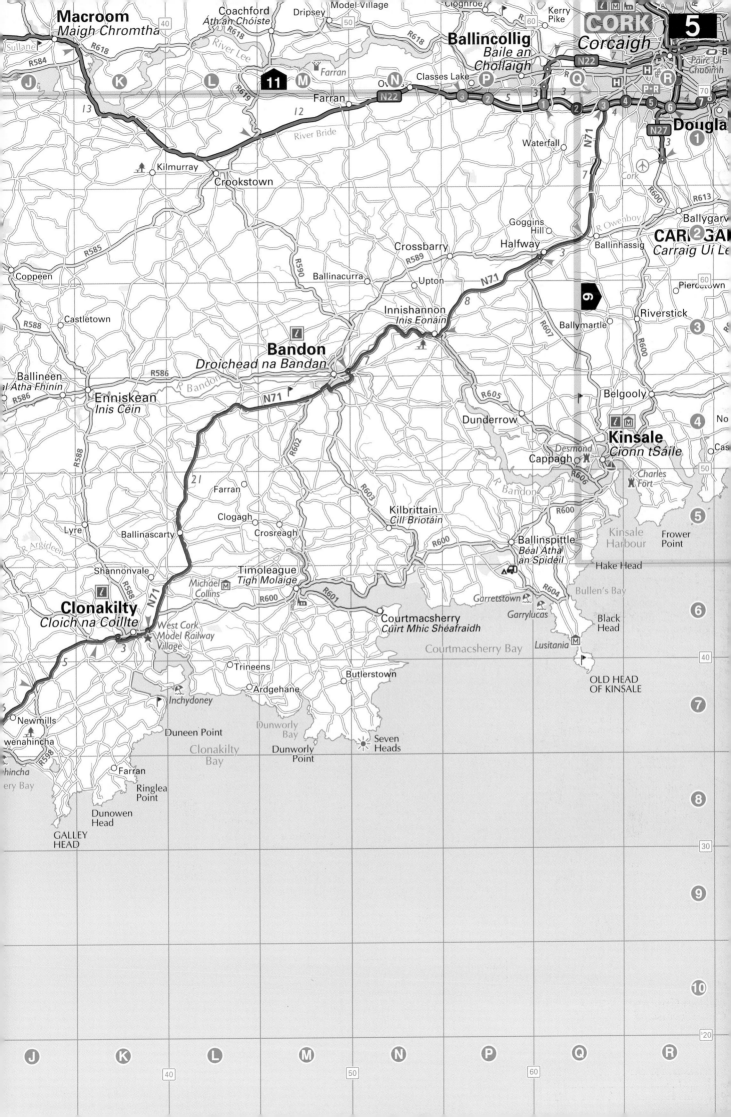

424 Knocknaskagh
Seefin
Farran
Castlelyons
Caisleán
Ó Liatháin
Rathcormac
Ráth Chormaic
Bridebridge

A   **B**   **C**   **D**   **E**   **F**   **G**   **H**

Glenville
Gleann an Phréacháin

16

Bartlemy

1   Farra   N20

Ardglass

M8 Toll

Grenagh   26

Watergrasshill
Cnocán na Biolraí

17
17

12

2   Whitechurch
Courtbrack

Carrignavar

R639   7

Lisgoold

Dungourney

11

18
18

Knockraha

3   Blarney
An Bhlárna
Ardamadane
Tweedmount   7

Sallybrook
Riverstown   Brooklodge

MIDLETON
Mainistir na Cor
Jameson
Experience

Tower
Cloghroe   Kerry
Pike

Glanmire
Gléann
Mhaghair   Glounthaune

N25

Churchtown

4   Ballincollig
Baile an
Chollaigh
CORK
Corcaigh

Blackrock   19   Little
Island   Courtstown   3   4

Carrigtwohill
Carraig Thuathail   Ballynacorra

asses Lake   N22   R608
3   3

N40   10   4

Fota
Wildlife Park

Douglas   N27

Passage West
An Pasáiste

Great Island

COBH
An Cóbh

Saleen

Cloyne
Cluain

5   Waterfall

Glenbrook

Cork Harbour
Cobh Heritage
Centre
Spike
Island

N28

Monkstown

R Owenboy

Ballygarvan

Shanbally   4

Ringaskiddy
Rinn an Scidigh

Whitegate
An Geata Bán

Ballyland

6   Goggins
Hill
Halfway   Ballinhassig   Coolmore
Cross
Crosshaven
Bun an Tábhairne
arry

N71

CARRIGALINE
Carraig Uí Leighin

Piercetown

Roche's
Point

Power
Head

Ringabella
Bay

7   non
náin
N71   8   R607   Ballymartle   Riverstick   Minane
Bridge

5   Belgooly

Roberts Cove

Robert's Head

Carrigadda
Bay

8   underrow   Nohoval
Castletown   Flat Head   Barry's Head   Roscoff
(Apr-Oct)
Santander
(May-Oct)

Kinsale
Kinsale
Cionn tSáile
Desmond
Cappagh   Charles
Fort

Newfoundland
Bay

9   n
áin
Ballinspittle
Béal Átha
an Spidéil   Kinsale
Harbour   Frower
Point

Hake Head

Bullen's Bay

10   sheri
Shéafraidh
Garretstown   Garrylucas
Lusitania   Black
Head

Courtmacsherry Bay   **OLD HEAD
OF KINSALE**

A   **B**   **C**   **D**   **E**   **F**   **G**   **H**

0   1   2   3   4   5 miles
0   1   2   3   4   5   6   7   8 km

Town plan: Cork p.71, Port plan: Ringaskiddy p.III

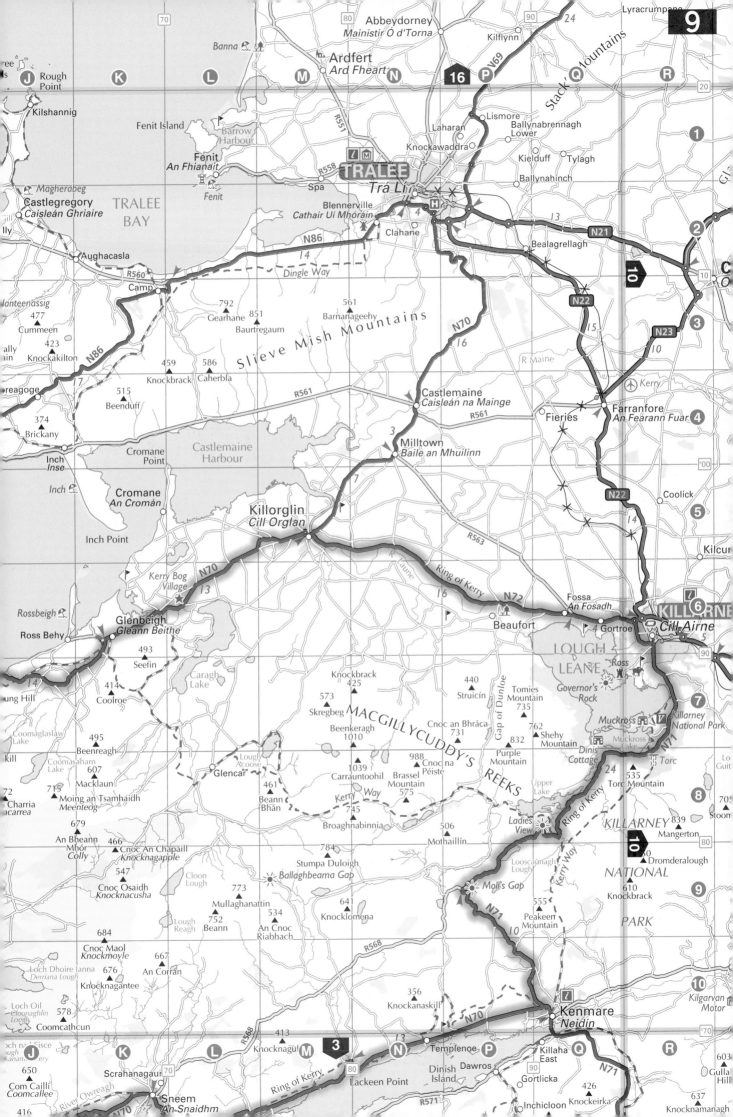

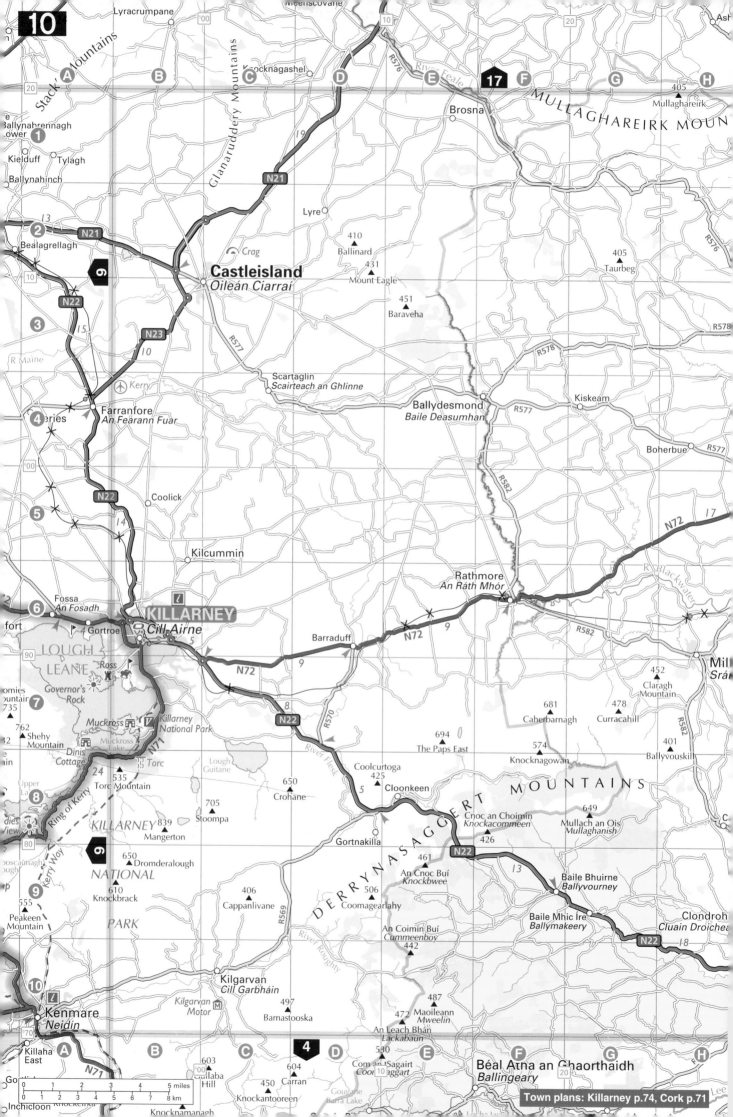

Lyracrumpane
Meenscovane
Ash

Stack Mountains
A
B
Glanaruddery Mountains
C
Knocknagashel
D
River Feale
E
17
F
G
Mullaghareirk
405
Mullaghareirk
H
MULLAGHAREIRK MOUN

Ballynabrennagh ower
1
Kielduff
Tylagh
Ballynahinch

Brosna

N21
2
13
N21
Bealagrellagh
N22
9
Crag
Castleisland
Oileán Ciarraí
410
Ballinard
431
Mount Eagle
405
Taurbeg
R576

3
15
N22
N23
10
R578
R578

R Maine
Kerry
Farranfore
An Fearann Fuar
eries
4
Scartaglin
Scairteach an Ghlinne
Ballydesmond
Baile Deasumhan
Kiskeam
R577

451
Baraveha
R582
Boherbue
R577

5
14
Coolick
N72
17

Kilcummin
Rathmore
An Ráth Mhór
R Blackwater
N72

Fossa
An Fosadh
6
KILLARNEY
Cill-Airne
Barraduff
N72
452
Claragh
Mountain
Mil
Srá

fort
4 Gortroe
5
9
681
Caherbarnagh
478
Curracahill
R582

LOUGH LEANE
Ross
90
Governor's Rock
N72
9
694
The Paps East
574
Knocknagowan
401
Ballyvouskill

omies untain
7
735
762
Shey Mountain
Muckross
Killarney
National Park
8
R570
MOUNTAINS

32
Muckross Lake
N71
River Flesk
Coolcurtoga
425
Cloonkeen
5

Dinis Cottage
Torc
535
Torc Mountain
Lough Guitane
650
Crohane
649
Mullach an Ois
Mullaghanish

Upper La
8
24
839
Stoompa
705
Cnoc an Choimín
Knockacommeen
426
Baile Bhuirne
Ballyvourney

dies View
Kerry Way
KILLARNEY
Mangerton
Gortnakilla
N22
13

9
650
Dromderalough
406
Cappanlivane
R569
461
An Cnoc Buí
Knockbwee
506
Coomagearlahy
Baile Mhic Íre
Ballymakeery
Clondroh
Cluain Droichea

80
9
NATIONAL
610
Knockbrack
DERRYNASAGGERT
N22
18

555
Peakeen Mountain
PARK
River Roughty
An Coimín Buí
Cummeenboy
442

ough
p
Kilgarvan
Cill Garbháin
Kilgarvan Motor
487
472
Maoileann Mweelin
Clondroh

10
Kenmare
Neidín
497
Barnastooska
530
An Leach Bhán
Lackabaun

Killaha East
A
N71
B
603
Gullaba Hill
C
604
Carran
4
D
Com Sagairt
Coo aggart
10
E
Béal Átna an Ghaorthaidh
Ballingeary
F
20
G
H

Gort
Inchicloon
Knocknagna
450
Knockantooreen
Gougane Barra Lake
Knocknamanagh

0 1 2 3 4 5 miles
0 1 2 3 4 5 6 7 8 km

Town plans: Killarney p.74, Cork p.71

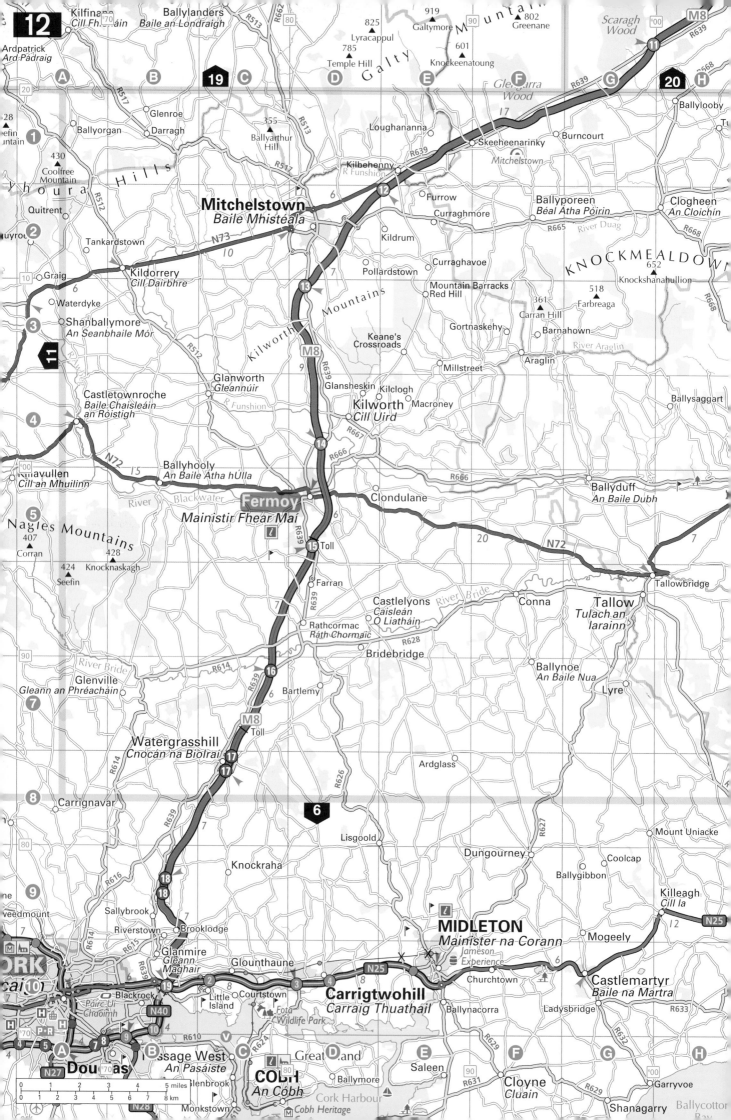

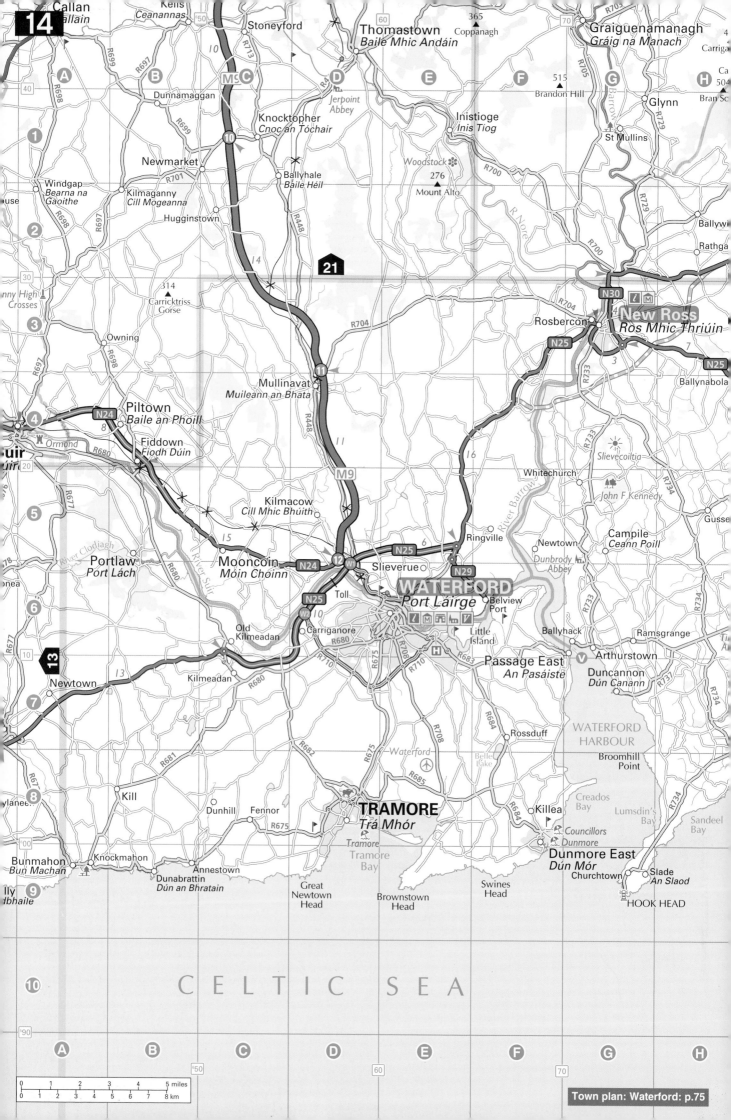

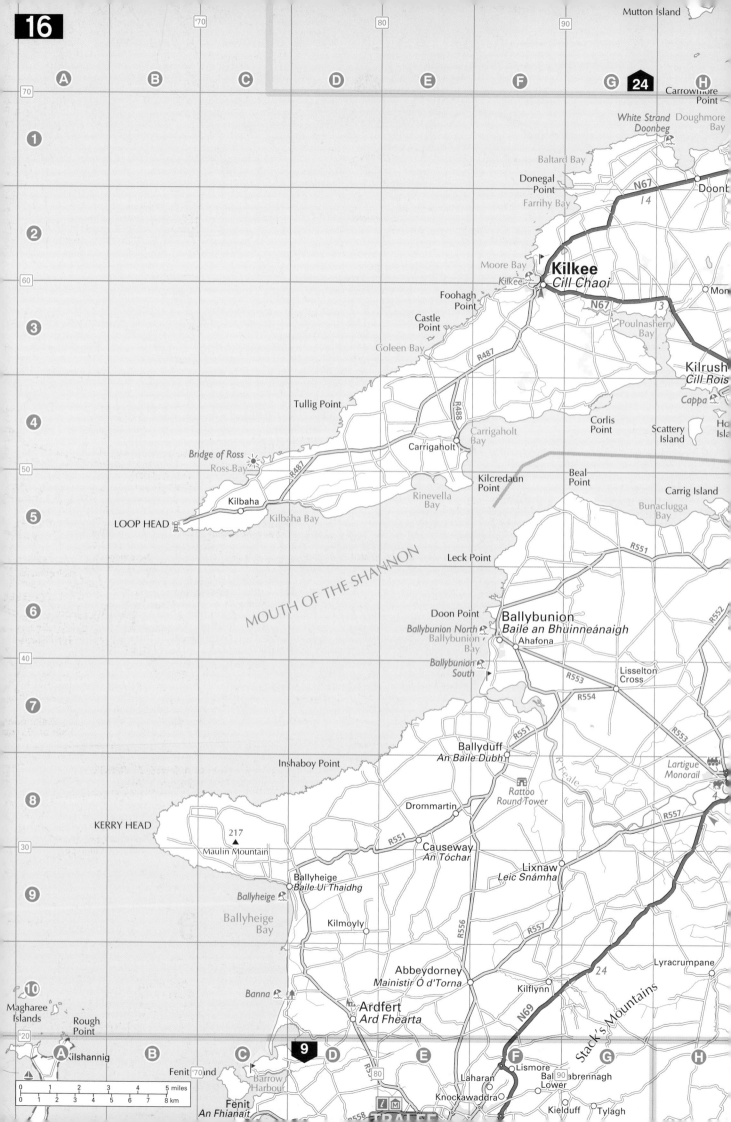

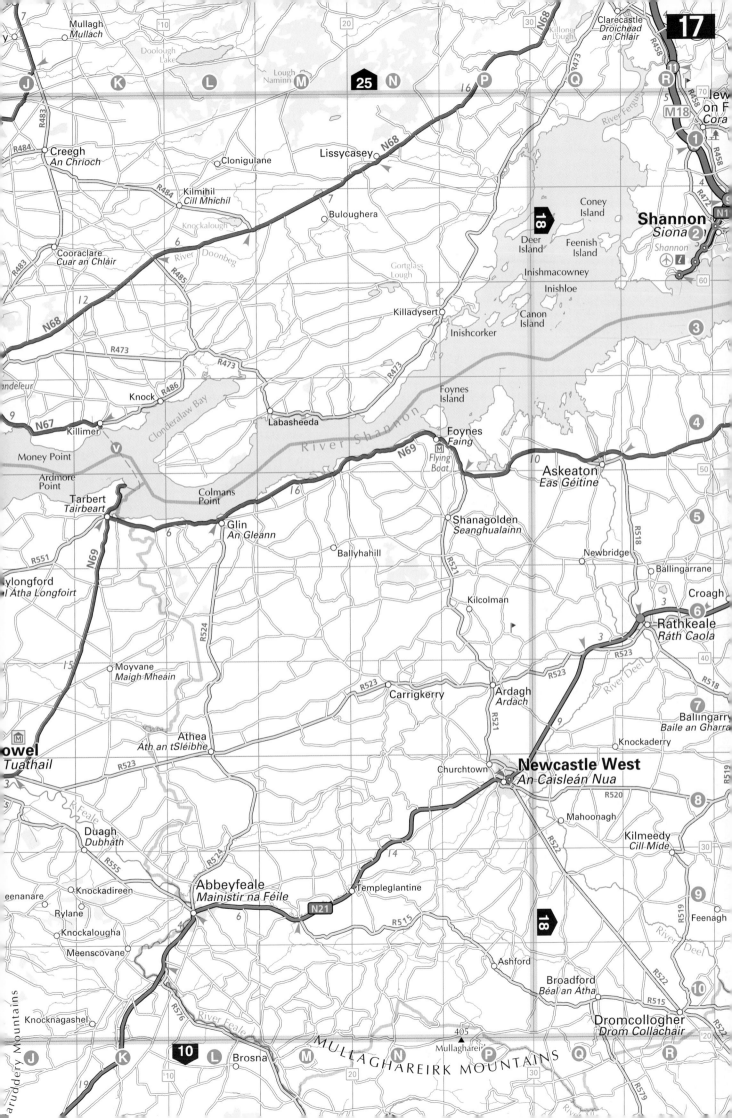

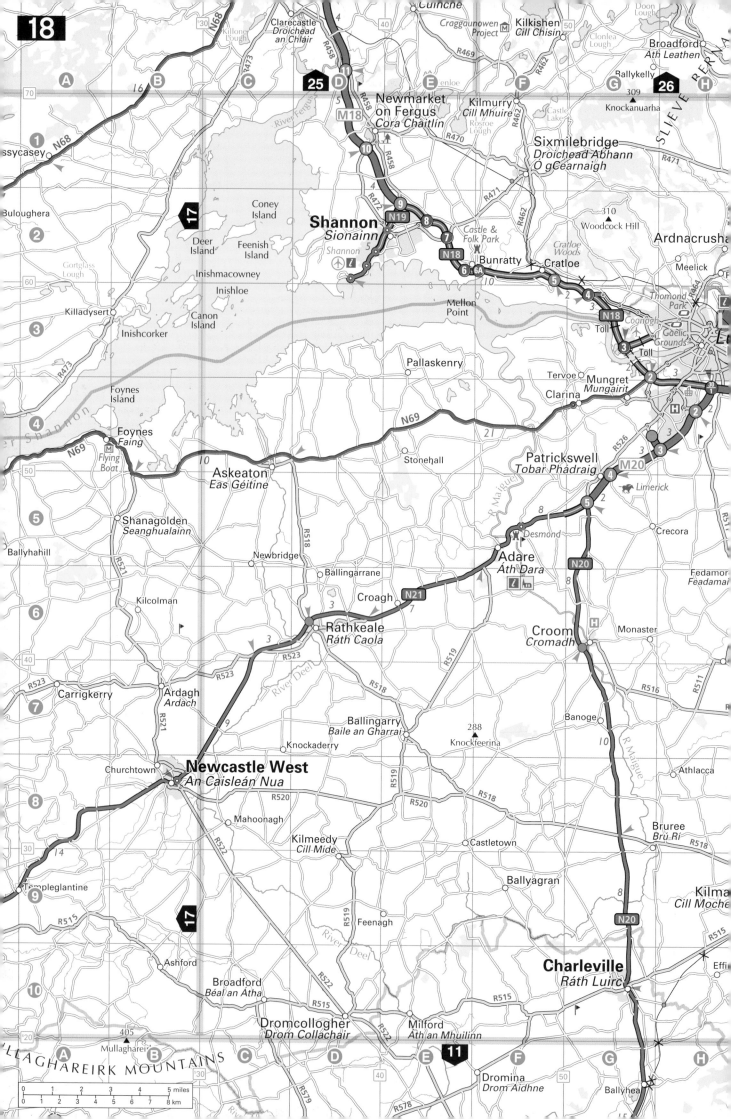

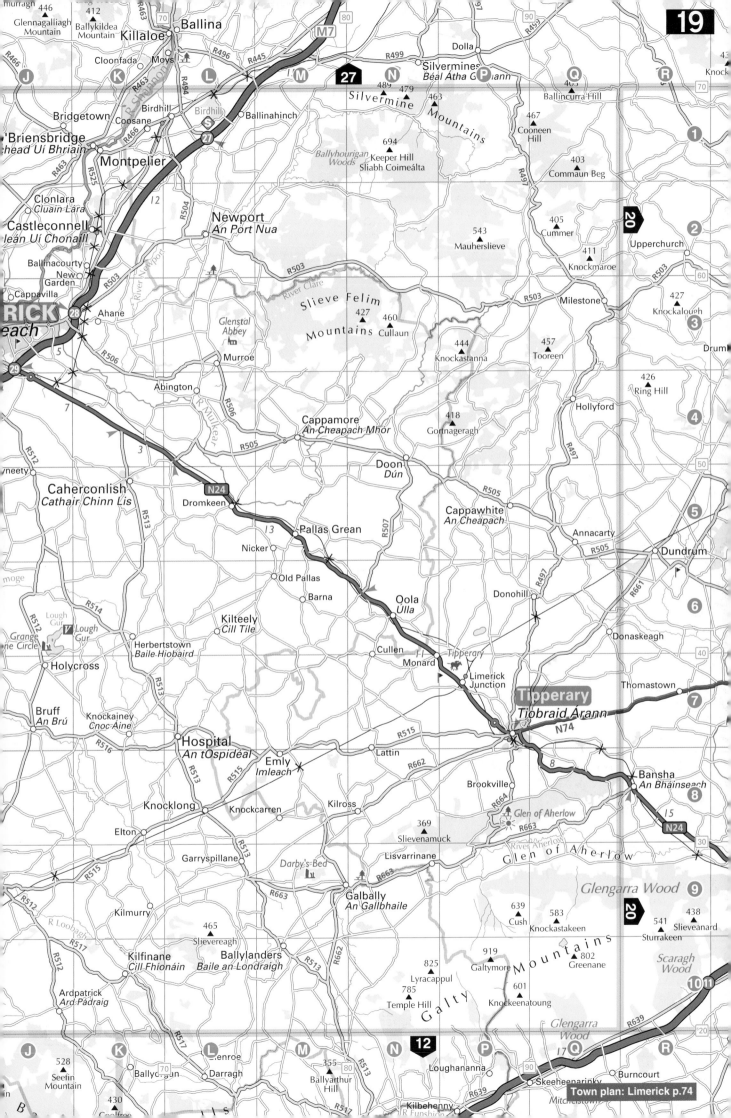

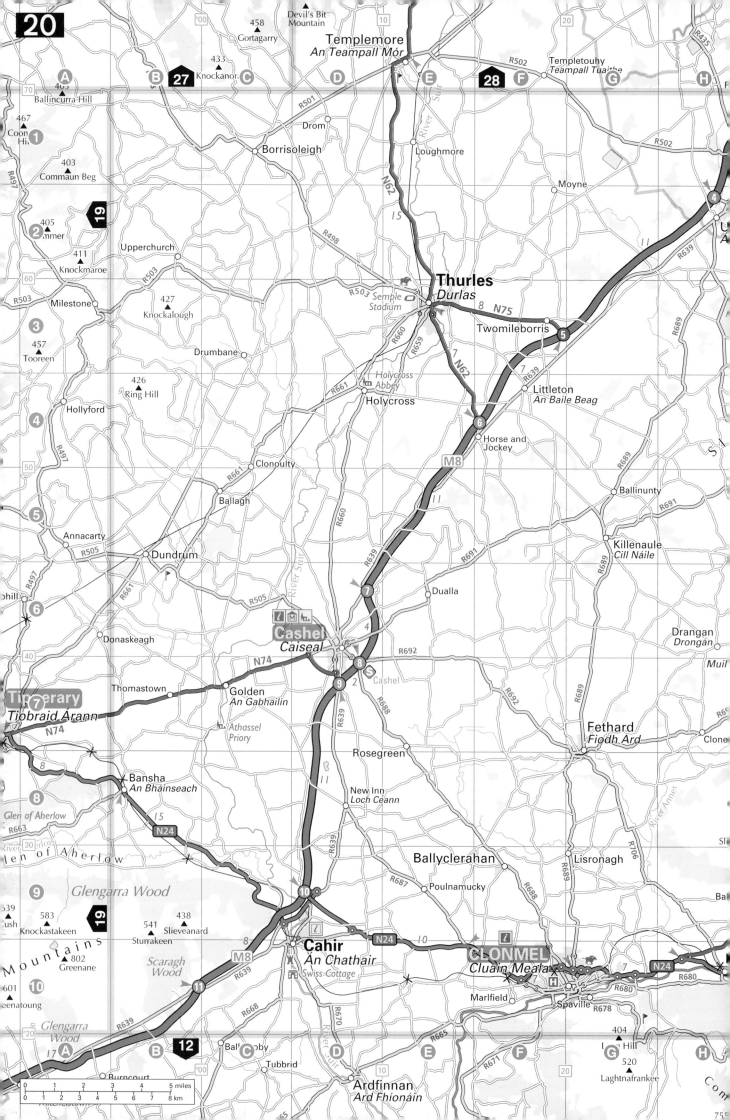

Tinahely
Tigh na hEille

606 ▲ Croghan
Kinsella

Ballyfad

31

ARKLOW
An tInbhear Mór

Arklow Head

Coolboy

Coolgreany
Cúil Ghréine

Kilmichael
Point

454 ▲

Inch
An Inis

Gorey

Kilanerin

Castletown

Monaseed

M11

Hollyfort

22

253 ▲
Tara Hill

Gorey
Guaire

Ballymoney

Ballymoney
North

Carnew
Carn an Bhua

R725

6

Craanford

23

Askamore

Courtown

Clough
An Chloch

420 ▲
Slieveboy

8

Courtown
Baile na Cúirte

Ballyduff

Riverchapel

Camolin
Cam Eolaing

Roney Point

10

Ballycanew
*Baile Uí
Chonnmhaí*

N11
rns
rna

Cloioge
Cloch Cúirte

R741

M11 due to
open 2019

Ballygarrett
Baile Ghearóid

Cahore
Cathóir

The Harrow
An Bráca

Boolavogue
Baile Mhaodhóg

Father
Murphy

Monamolin

Ballyedmond

R742

Monagear
Móin na gCaor

Oulart
An tAbhállort

Kilmuckridge
Cill Mhucraise

Morriscastle

ORTHY
idh

R744

Ballaghkeen

Glenbrien

R741

R744

Blackwater
An Abhainn Dubh

R742

llymurn
ate
lán na nGabhar

Screen

15

Ballnesker

WEXFORD
BAY

Curracloe

R743

Curracloe

Crossabeg

Castlebridge
Dróichead an Chaisleáin

Wexford
Wildfowl

Raven
Point

WEXFORD
Loch Garman

The Raven
Point

Wexford Harbour

J
N25

Rosslare
Point

Irish
Agricultural

Fishguard
Pembroke

[handwritten notes:] Get off at extension 22 to onto R772

Get off at extension 23. south towards Ferns

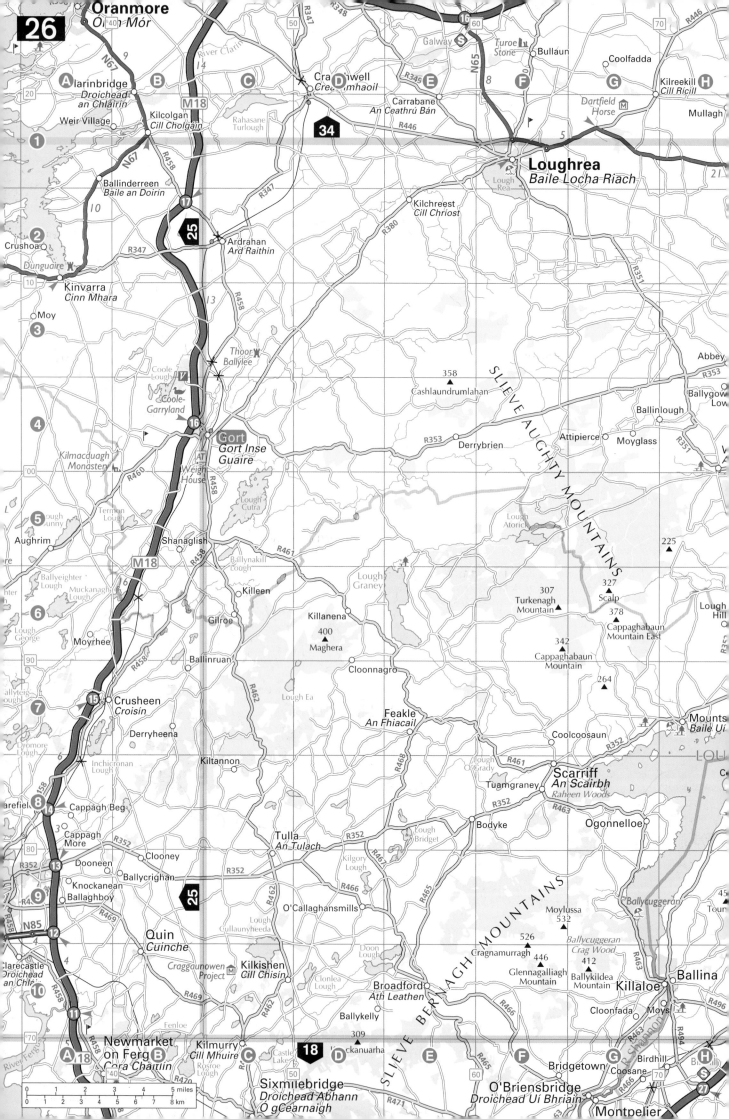

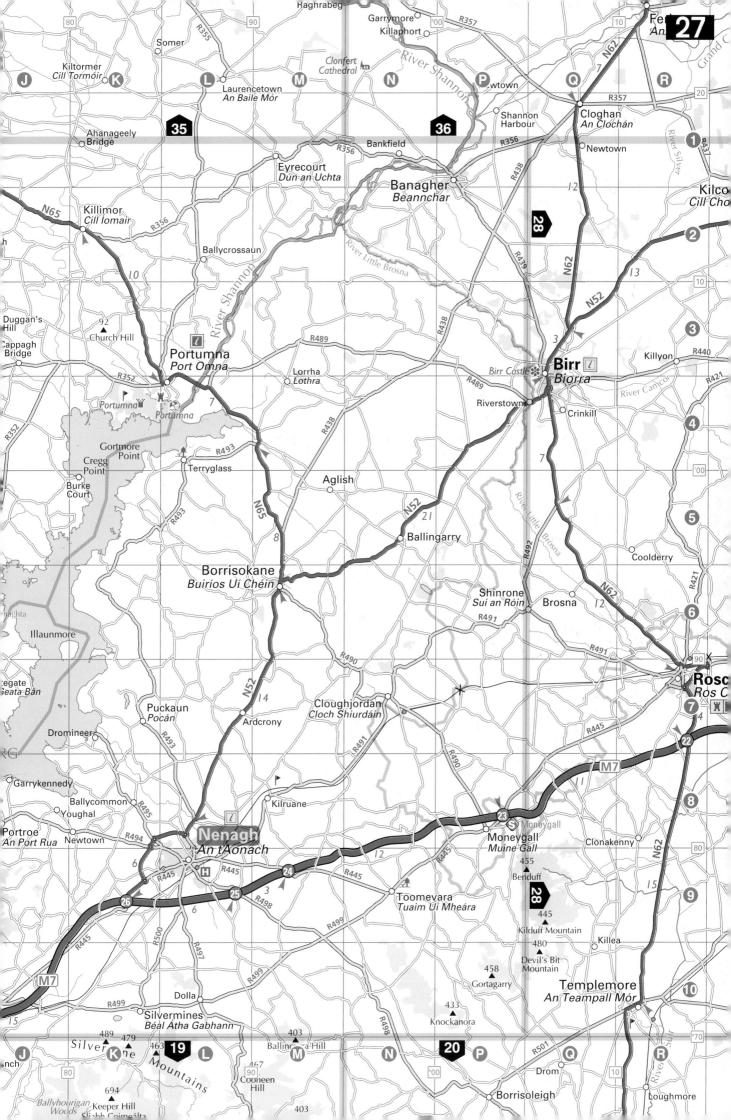

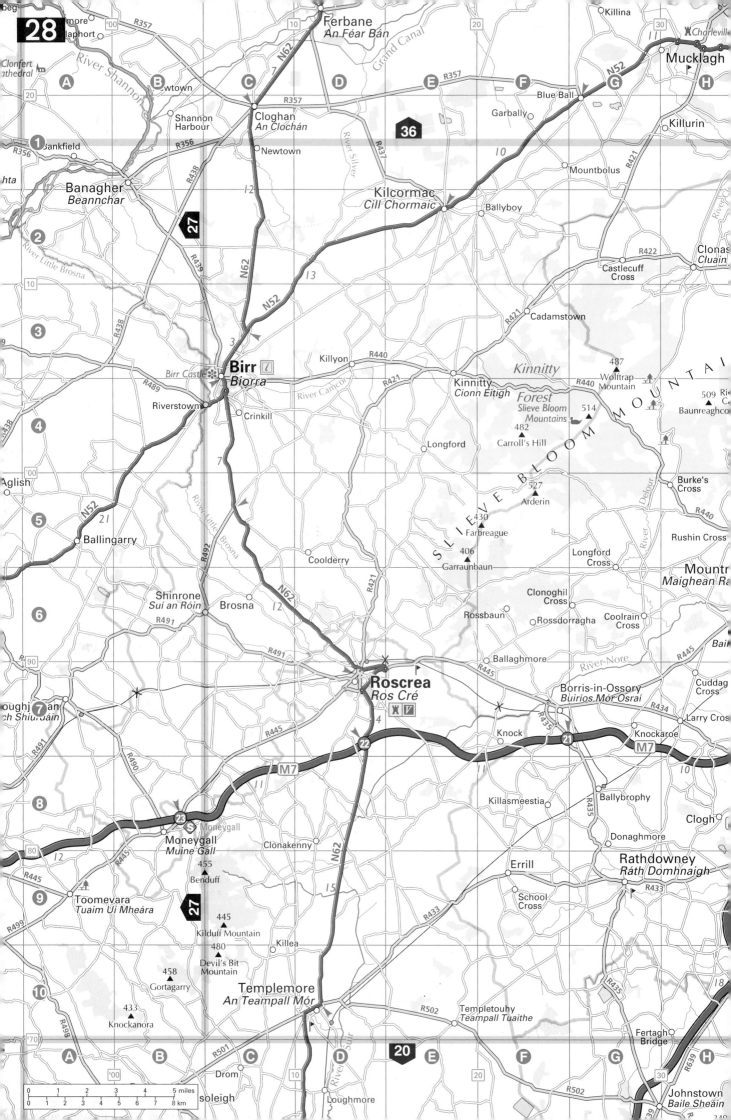

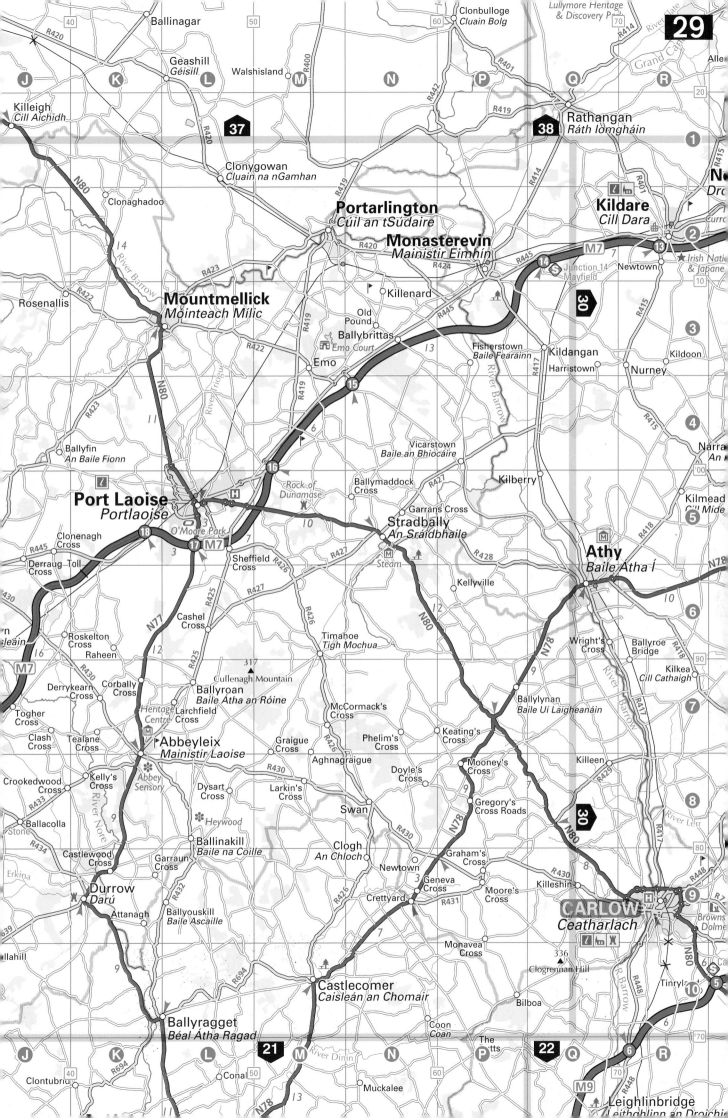

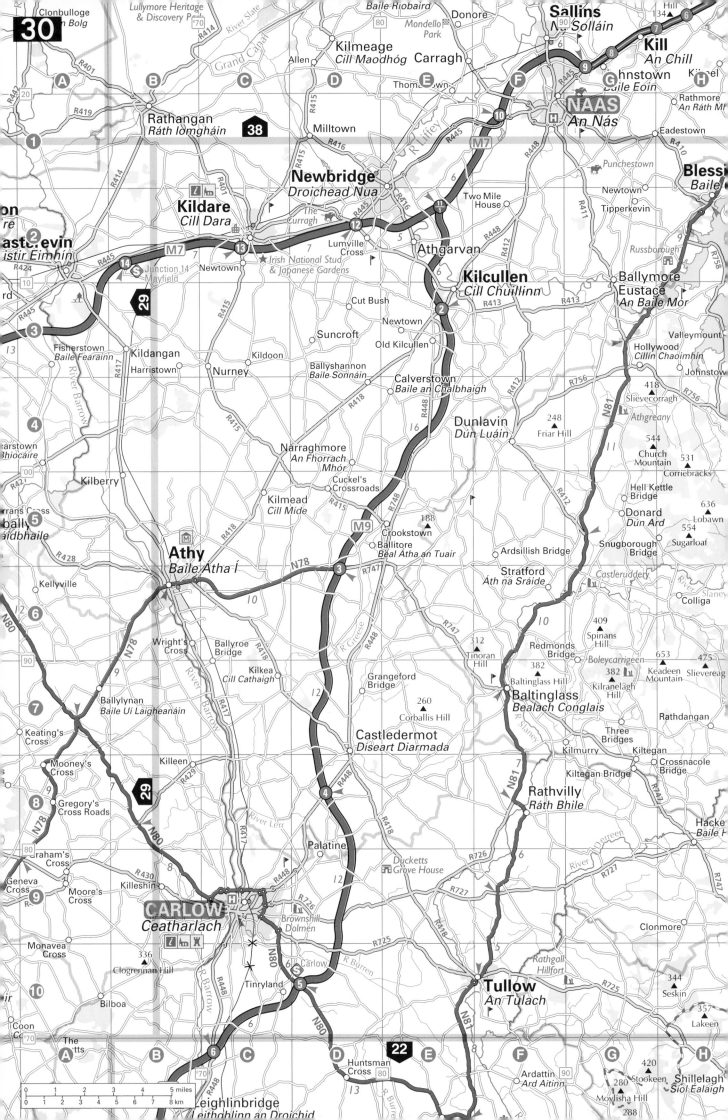

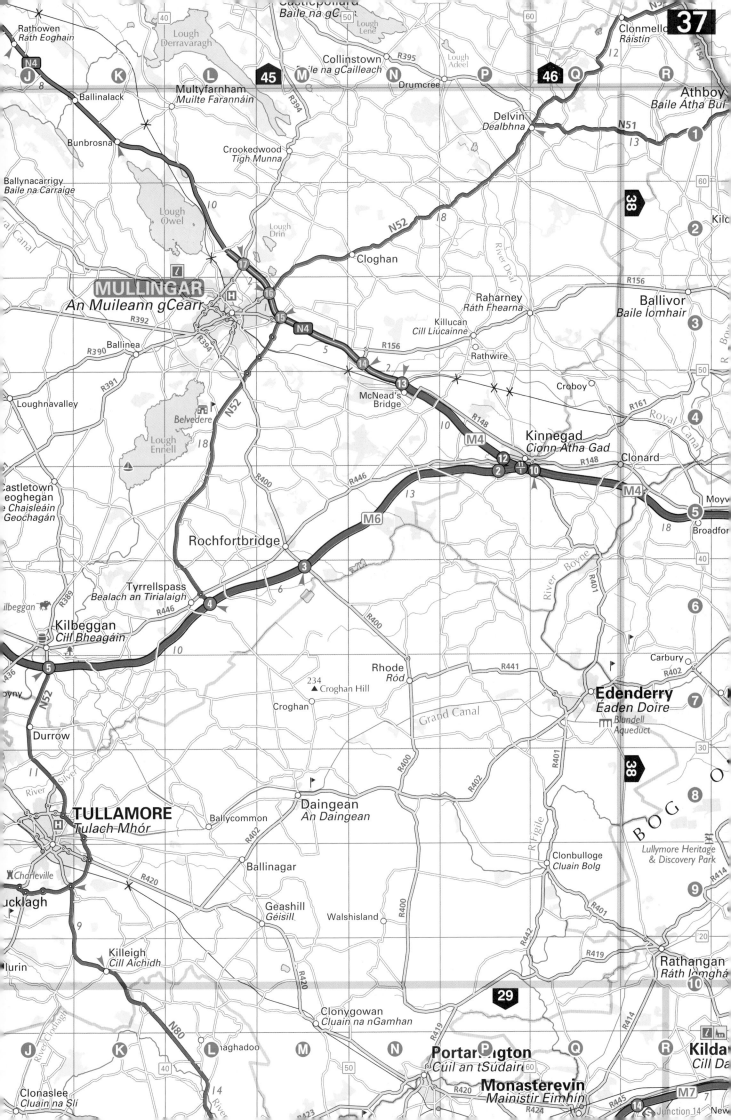

Blacksod

Dumha Dhearc
Dooyork

N59

A   B   Dubhoiléan Mór   C   D   E   F   G   H
Duvillaun More

An Ceann Ramhar
Kinrovar

Dumha Thuama
Doohooma

Srahnamanragh

48

Ballycroy

Ballycroy
National
Park

1

10

Silverstrand
Dugort   Golden

Saddle Head   **ACHILL ISLAND**
ACAILL   671 ▲
Slievemore   Dugort

Tóin an tSeanbhaile
Tonatanvally

Dún Ibhir
Dooniver

2

ACHILL HEAD   688 ▲   Dooagh   Keel   Keel
664 ▲   *Dumha Acha*   *An Caol*   *An Caol*

Pollagh   Bun an Churraigh
Bunacurry

Keel   Keel
Lough

R319

Inis Bigil
Inishbiggle

Annagh
Island

14

N59

Keem   Keel

An Caiseal
Cashel

3

466 ▲
An Mionnán
Minaun

R319

452 ▲
Owenduff
Hill

Lough
Gall

Dumha Éige
Dooega

337 ▲
An Cnoc
Mór
Knockmore

Loch na
Sraithíní
*Sraheens
Lough*

Gob an Choire
Achill Sound

An Corrán
Corraun Peninsula

4

Ceann Dumha Éige
Dooega Head

Dooega

524 ▲   541 ▲

286 ▲
Derreen

Cnoc an
Chorráin
Corraun Hill

Gobán
Gubbaun Poi

Kildavnet ✗

Achill Sound

5

Acaill Bheag
Achillbeg Island

90

Clare Island

CLEW   BAY

6

Clare Island

Knockmore
462 ▲

Clare Island

Old Head

Carrowmore

7

Portnakilly

P

80

Roonah Quay

Louisburgh
Cluain Cearbán

R378

8

P

Caher Island

Roonagh
Lough

River B

9

Inishturk
Inis Toirc   191 ▲
Inishturk

Killeen

R335   580

Inishdalla

70

Ben Bury
795

Doo
Lough

Ba

10

Inishbofin
Inis Bó Finne

Davillaun

Inishdegilmore

803

814
Mweelrea   ▲

495 ▲

Mweelrea Mountains

Inishark
Inis Airc

Crump
Island

Coonaluinga

A   B   ...lyon   C   D   E   F   Cloonagh   G   Cappagowlaun   H
Renvyle
Point   Townacurra

333 ▲

32

Inishgort

70   Tully Cross

581 ▲
Benchoona   Binn Mhór

0 1 2 3 4 5 miles
0 1 2 3 4 5 6 7 8 km   P

356 ▲
Tully

Garraun   598 ▲

Lough Fee

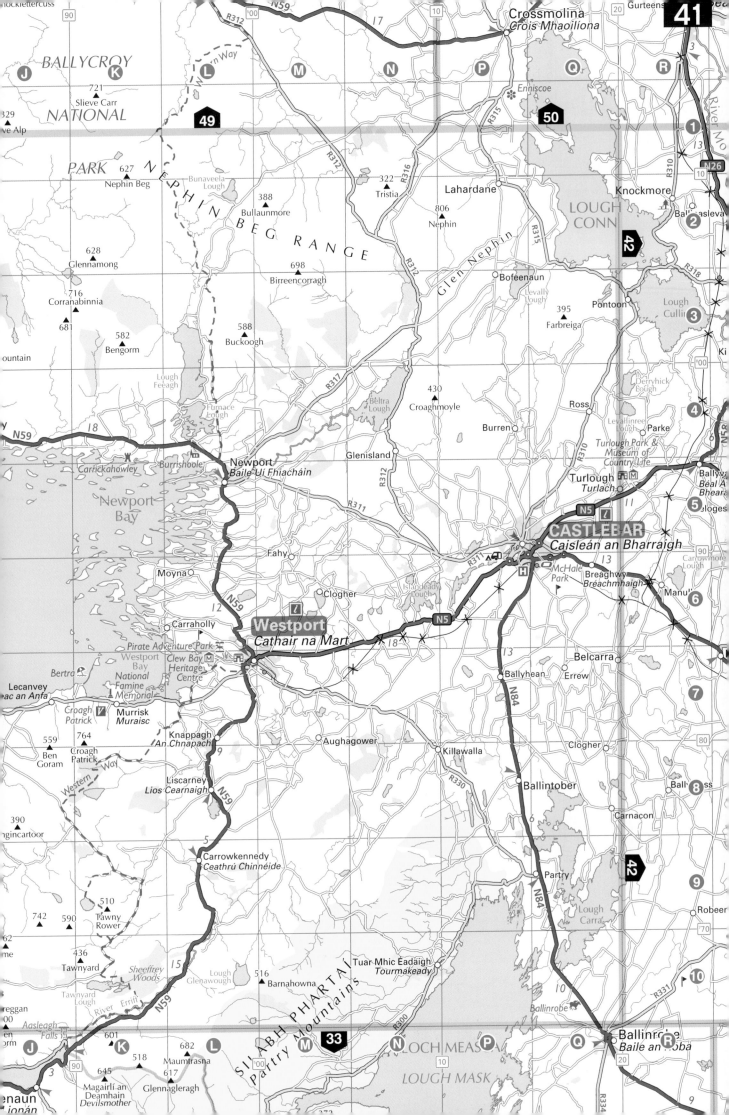

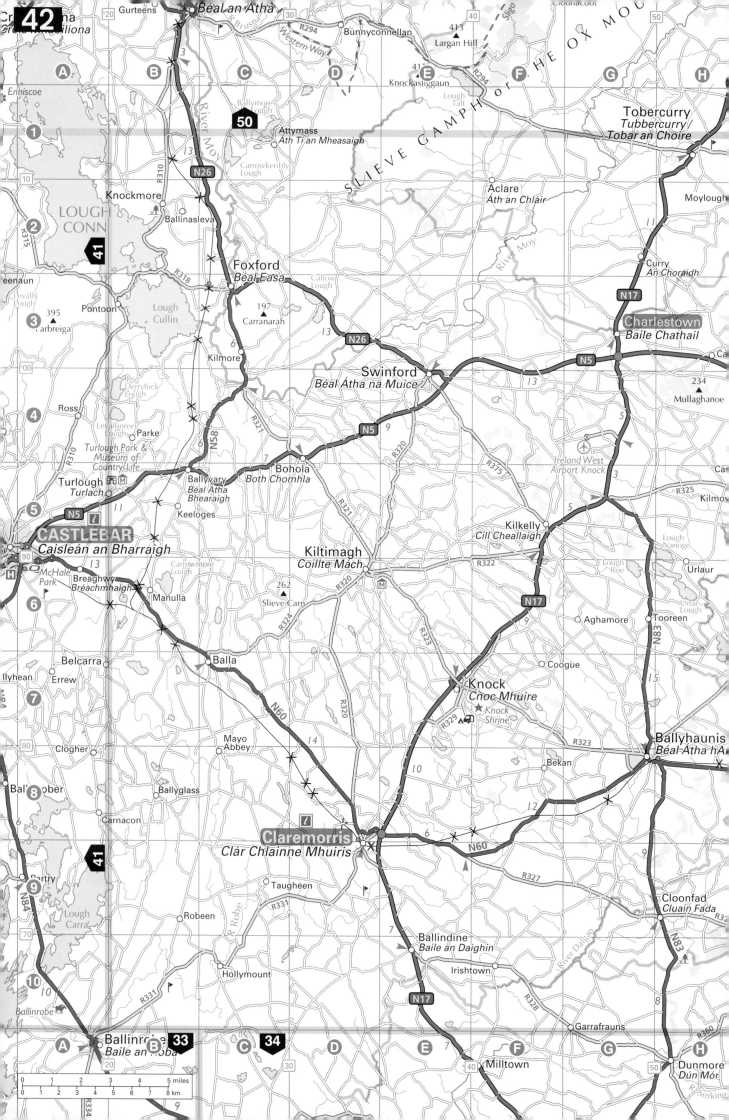

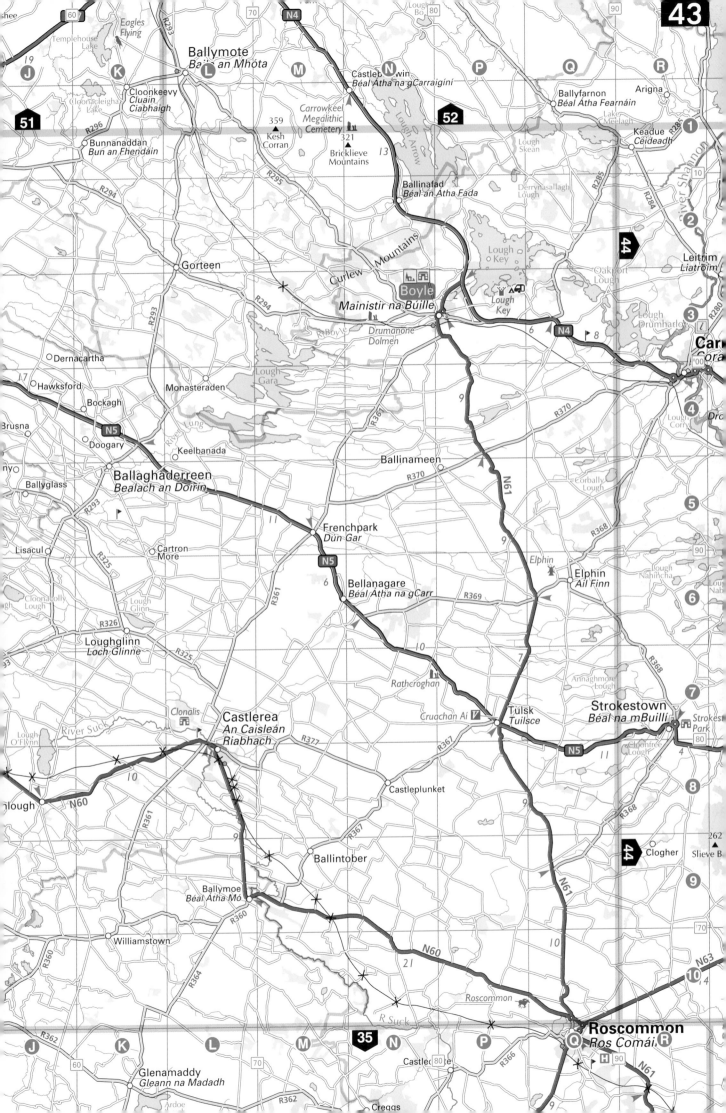

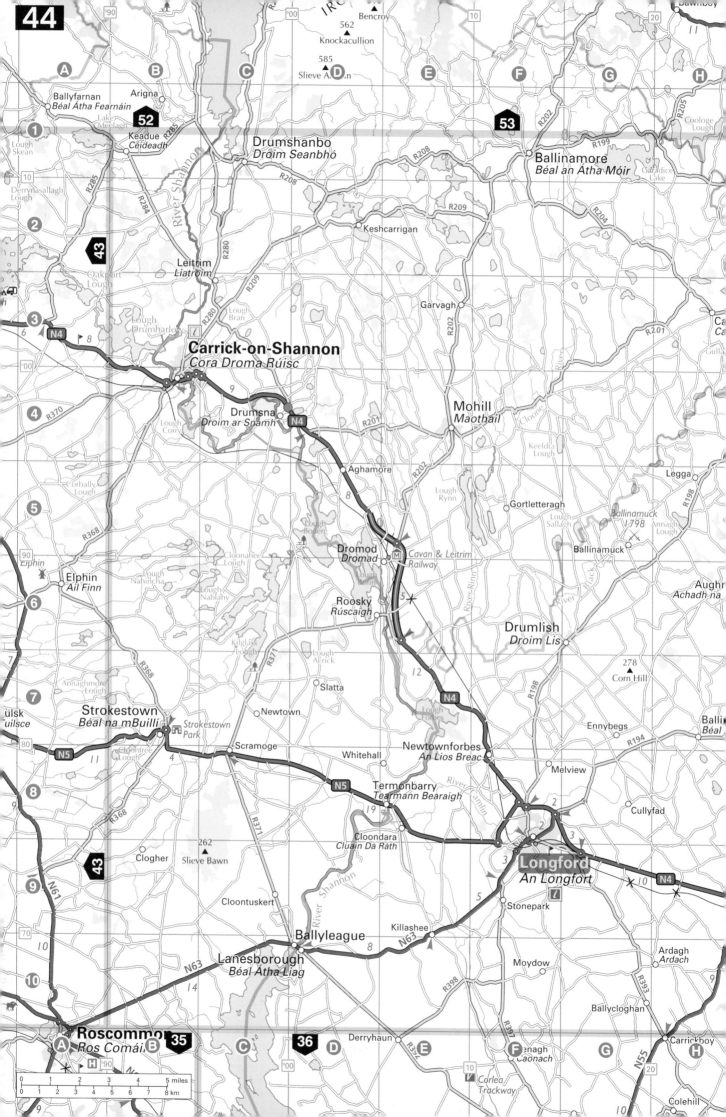

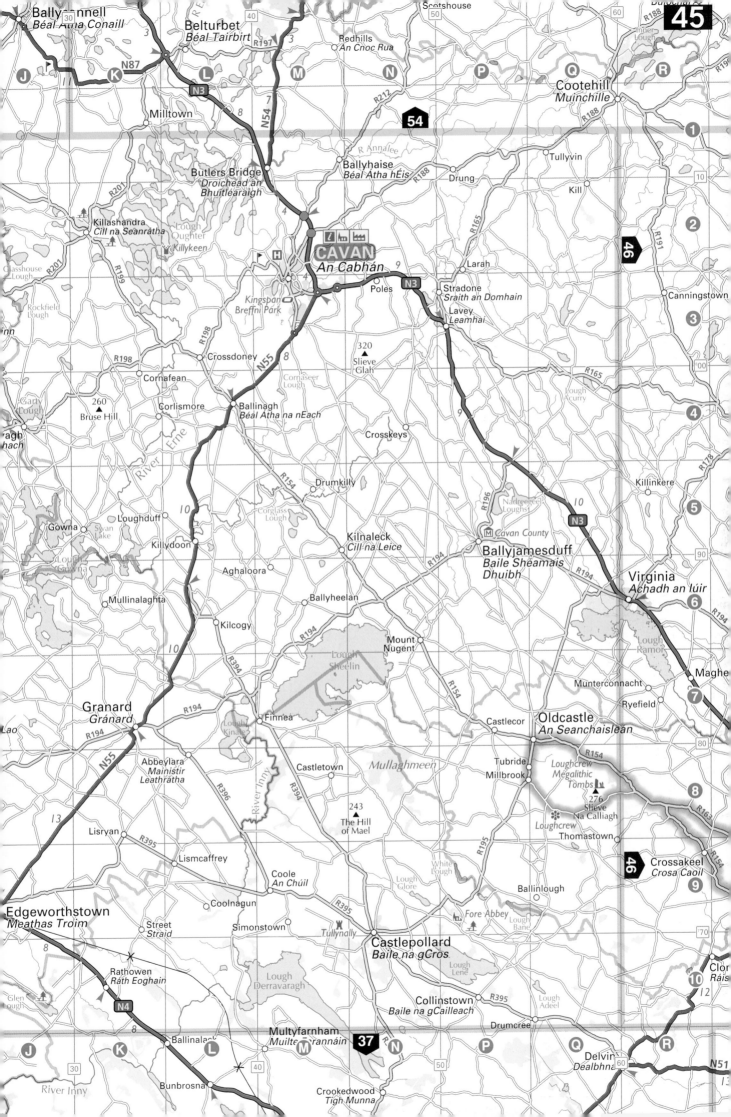

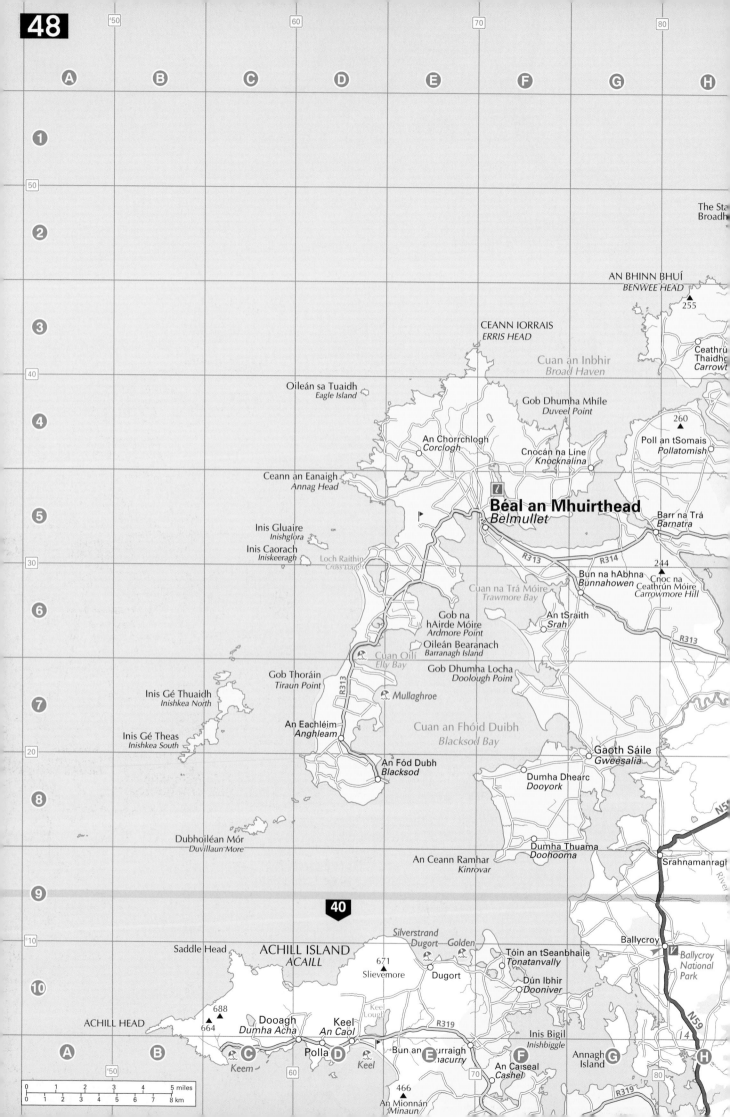

The Sta
Broadh

AN BHINN BHUÍ
BENWEE HEAD
▲ 255

CEANN IORRAIS
ERRIS HEAD

Ceathrú
Thaidhg
Carrowt

Cuan an Inbhir
Broad Haven

Oileán sa Tuaidh
Eagle Island

Gob Dhumha Mhíle
Duveel Point

An Chorrchlogh
Corclogh

Cnocán na Line
Knocknalina

Poll an tSomais
Pollatomish
▲ 260

Ceann an Eanaigh
Annag Head

Béal an Mhuirthead
Belmullet

Barr na Trá
Barnatra

Inis Gluaire
Inishglora

R313   R314   244
▲

Inis Caorach
Iniskeeragh

Loch Raithin
Cross Lough

Bun na hAbhna
Bunnahowen

Cnoc na
Ceathrún Móire
Carrowmore Hill

Cuan na Trá Móire
Trawmore Bay

An tSraith
Srah

Gob na
hAirde Móire
Ardmore Point

Oileán Bearanach
Barranagh Island

Gob Dhumha Locha
Doolough Point

Cuan Oilí
Elly Bay

Gob Thoráin
Tiraun Point

R313

Mullaghroe

Inis Gé Thuaidh
Inishkea North

An Eachléim
Anghleam

Cuan an Fhóid Duibh
Blacksod Bay

Gaoth Sáile
Gweesalia

Inis Gé Theas
Inishkea South

An Fód Dubh
Blacksod

Dumha Dhearc
Dooyork

Dubhoiléan Mór
Duvillaun More

Dumha Thuama
Doohooma

An Ceann Ramhar
Kinrovar

Srahnamanragh

▼ **40**

Silverstrand
Dugort — Golden

Ballycroy

Saddle Head

ACHILL ISLAND
ACAILL

671
Slievemore

Dugort

Tóin an tSeanbhaile
Tonatanvally

Ballycroy
National
Park

Dún Ibhir
Dooniver

ACHILL HEAD

688
▲
664 ▲

Dooagh
Dumha Acha

Keel
An Caol

Keel
Lough

R319

Inis Bigil
Inishbiggle

Polla

Keel

Bun an
urraigh
acurry

An Caiseal
Cashel

Annagh
Island

N59

466
An Mionnán
Minaun

R319

0 1 2 3 4 5 miles
0 1 2 3 4 5 6 7 8 km

J   K   L   M   N   P   Q   R

DOWNPATRICK
HEAD

229

304
Glinsce
Glinsk

Bunatrahir
Bay   Boytown

R314

340
An Tamhnach Mhór
Tawnaghmore

Céide Fields

Ballycastle
Baile an Chàisil

Luachair Ghlas
Lougherglass

379
Mám an Cheo
Maumakeogh

Lackan
Bay

Western Way

River Ballinglen

237
Aghaleague

Gleann na
Muaidhe
Glenamoy

River Glenamoy

Rathfran
Bay

River Cloonaghmore

Ross Killala

K

Killala
Cill Ala

Bart
Islan

R314

335
Slieve Fyagh

R315

50

269
Carrafull
Bangor Erris
Baingear

Oweninny
Bog

AT

River Oweniny

Cloonagh
Lough

370
Knocklettercuss

14

River Owenmore

Bellacorick

N59

R312

Lough
Dahybaun

17

N59

12 Ardoughan

Gurteens

BA
Béa

BALLYCROY

Western Way

Crossmolina
Crois Mhaoilíona

329
ve Alp

NATIONAL

721
Slieve Carr

Enniscoe

R315

River Mo

9
13

R310

PARK

627

Nephin Beg

NEPHIN

Bunaveela
Lough

41

R312

322
Tristia

R316

Lahardane

806
Nephin

Knockmore

N26

R310

10
Ballinasleva

628
Glennamong

388
Bullaunmore

BEG

RANGE

LOUGH
CONN

716
Corranabinnia

90

681

582
Bengorm

588
Buckoogh

698
Birreencorragh

Glen Nephin

R315

Bofeenaun

Levally
Lough

395
Farbreiga

Pont
20

Lough
Cullin

R318

J   K   L   M   N   P   Q   R

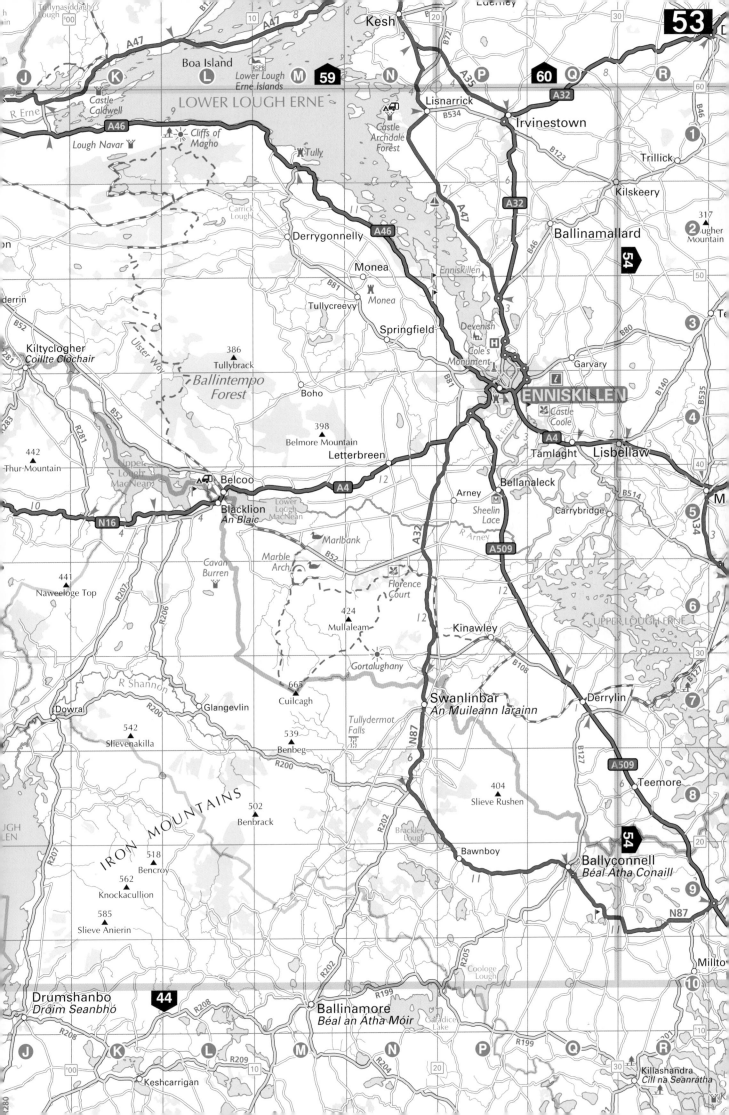

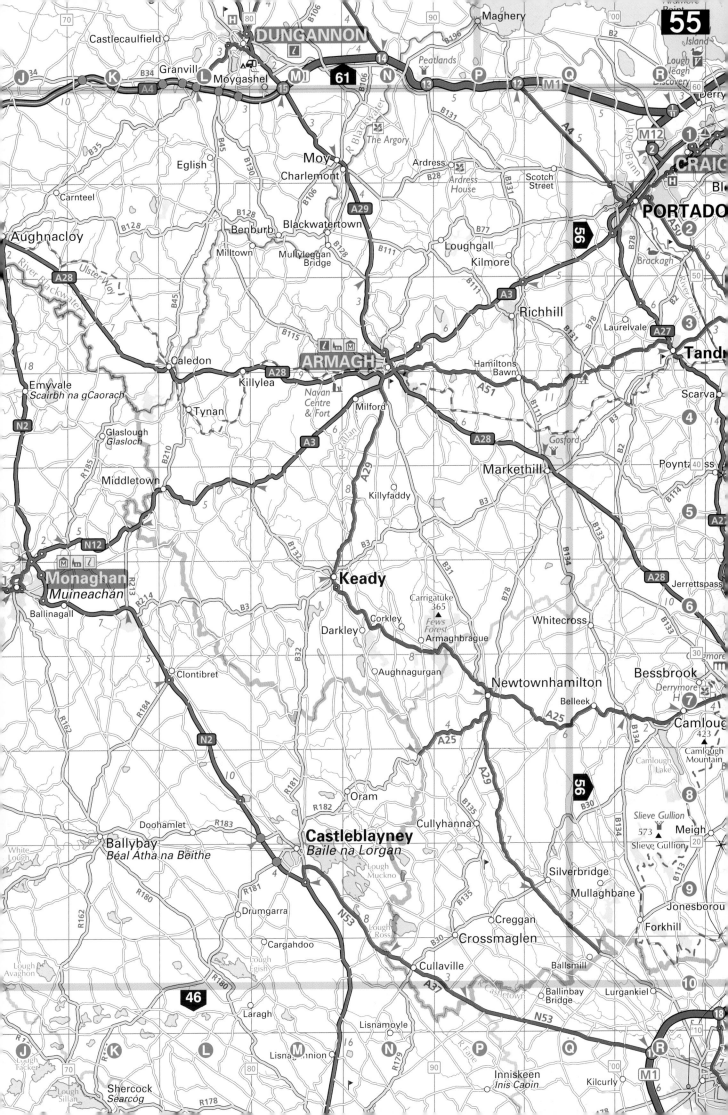

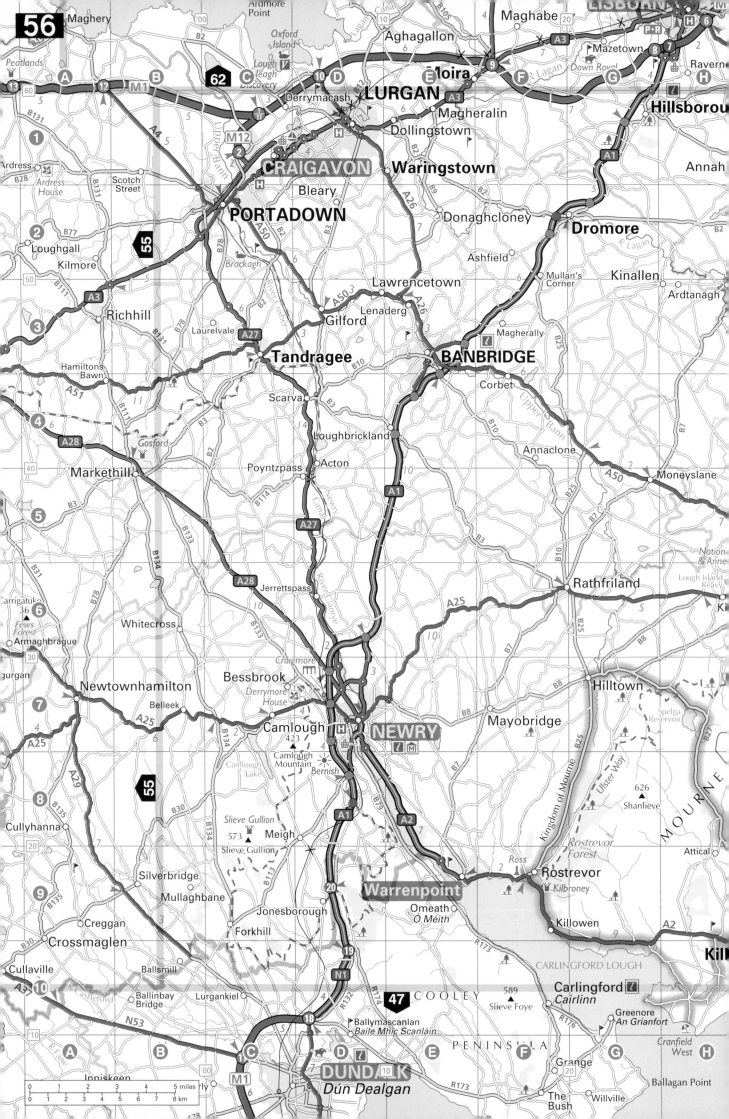

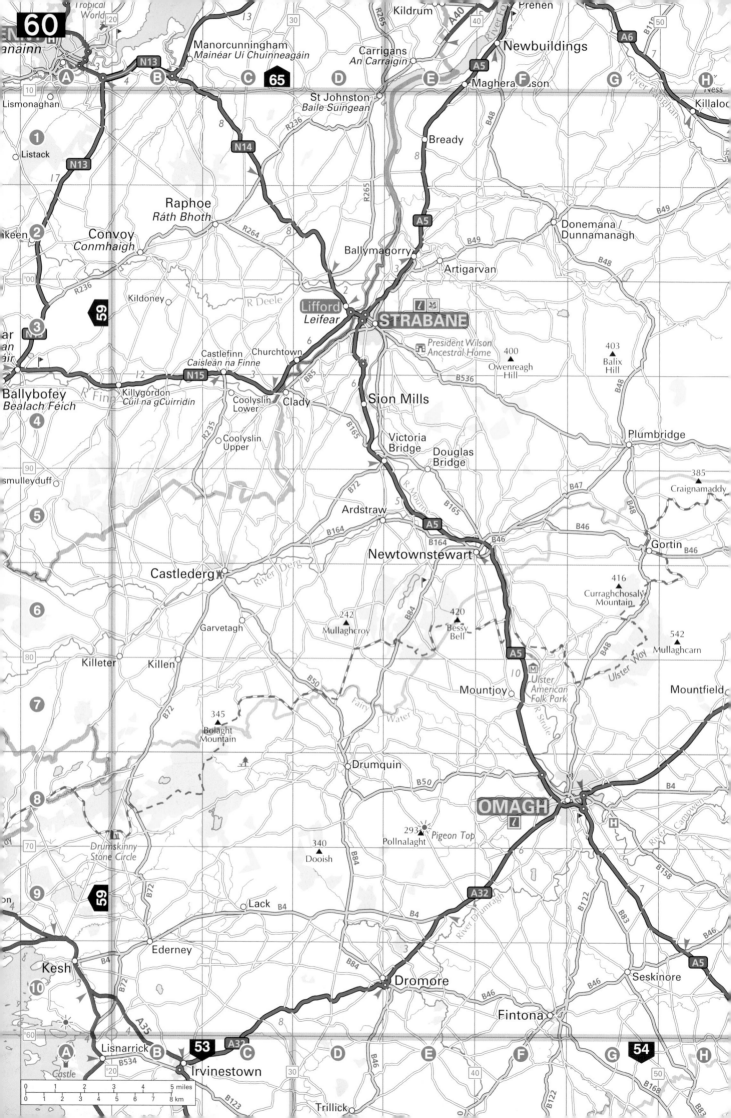

J K L M N P Q R

Ulster Way

A2

Ballygally

Carncastle

Old Mill
Carnfunnock
Drains Bay
B148

LARNE H

474
Agnew's Hill
Millbrook
Kilwaughter
3

Glynn

Magheramorne

A8
B100

Raloo Glenoe

Ballynure B58 B99

Straid

Ulster Way

312
Slievetrue

B90

Ballycarry

Ballystrudder
Blackhead

Whitehead

Cairnryan

Skernaghan
Point

Isle of Muck

Islandmagee

The Gobbins

CARRICKFERGUS

Greenisland

BELFAST LOUGH

Cairnryan

Douglas (Apr-Sept)

Liverpool (Birkenhead)

Lighthouse
Island

Mew
Island

Copeland
Island

Foreland
Point

Helen's
Bay
Crawfords
burn

NEWTOWNABBEY

BANGOR

Groomsport

Ulster Folk
& Transport

Crawfordsburn

Belfast's
Window
on Wildlife
RSPB

HOLYWOOD

Conlig
Balloo
Wetland

A48

A21

Donaghadee

Ifast
Zoo

Cave
Hill
A55

George Best
Belfast City

M2
M5

A2
1B
1A

Stormont
(Parliament Buildings)

B170

217
Cairngaver

Somme
Heritage
Centre

The Ark
Open Farm

B172

Millisle

P+R

A55

Lisnabreeny

A20

DUNDONALD

A22

Kiltonga
Scrabo
Scrabo
Tower

Ballybarnes

NEWTOWNARDS

Newtownards

Carrowdore

Cardy

8

Comber

Crossnacreevy

Mount Stewart
House & Gardens

Greyabbey

Ballywalter

B5

Knockbracken

Moneyreagh
B178

Carryduff

Drumbo

A24

A23

B103

Lagan
Valley

B23

Temple
B6

A21

A22

Ballygowan

Lisbane

Balloo Killinchy

Chapel
Island
Reagh
Island

South
Island

Mahee
Island

**STRANGFORD
LOUGH**

**ARDS
PENINSULA**

Kircubbin

Glastry

Ballyhalbert

Portavogie

J K **Sa**ltfield M **57** N P Q R

A24

Darragh
Cross

Kirkistown

Rowallane
Garden

Town plans
Belfast............................70
Cork...............................71
Dublin............................72–73
Galway...........................71
Kilkenny.........................74
Killarney.........................74
Limerick..........................74
Londonderry Derry.........75
Sligo...............................75
Waterford.......................75

Port plans
Belfast............................III
Dublin Port.....................III
Larne..............................III
Ringaskiddy....................III
Rosslare Europort..........III

Key to town plans
Eochair

Mótarbhealach saor ó dholaí (NI)	**M3**	Toll-free motorway (NI)
Príomhbhealach náisiúnta (IRL)	**N4**	National primary route (IRL)
Príomhbhealach (NI)	**A12**	Primary route (NI)
Bealach náisiúnta tánaisteach (IRL)	**N69**	National secondary route (IRL)
Bóthar A (NI)	**A501**	A road (NI)
Bóthar réigiúnach (IRL)	**R118**	Regional road (IRL)
Bóthar B (NI)	**B123**	B road (NI)
Bóthar eile		Other road
Bóthar rochtana teoranta		Restricted access road
Ceantar coisithe		Pedestrian zone
Cosán		Footpath
Bealach fithiseach istigh		Inner orbital route
Bealach fithiseach seachtrach		Outer orbital route
Sráid aon-bhealach, geata/bacainn		One-way street, gate/barrier
Carrchlós, stáisiún bus	P	Car park, bus station
Iarnród éadrom/tram		Light railway/tram

Foirgneamh spéisiúil	College	Building of interest
Ospidéal, le hAonad Timpistí & Éigeandála	H H	Hospital, with Accident & Emergency
Eaglais nó séipéal	†	Church or chapel
Leithris		Toilet
Ionad eolais turasóireachta, ionad cuairteoirí nó oidhreachta		Tourist information, visitor or heritage centre
Ionad siopadóireachta, shopmobility		Shopping centre, shopmobility
National Trust (NI), An Taisce (IRL)	AT	National Trust site (NI/IRL)
Leabharlann, oifig an phoist		Library, post office
Músaem, caisleán		Museum, castle
Séadchomhartha nó dealbh, balla cathrach	•	Monument or statue, city wall
Galfchúrsa		Golf course
Amharclann, pictiúrlann		Theatre, cinema
Drioglann nó grúdlann		Distillery or brewery
Ionad amhairc		Viewpoint
Páirc nó spás oscailte, reilig		Park or open space, cemetery
Coillearnach		Woodland

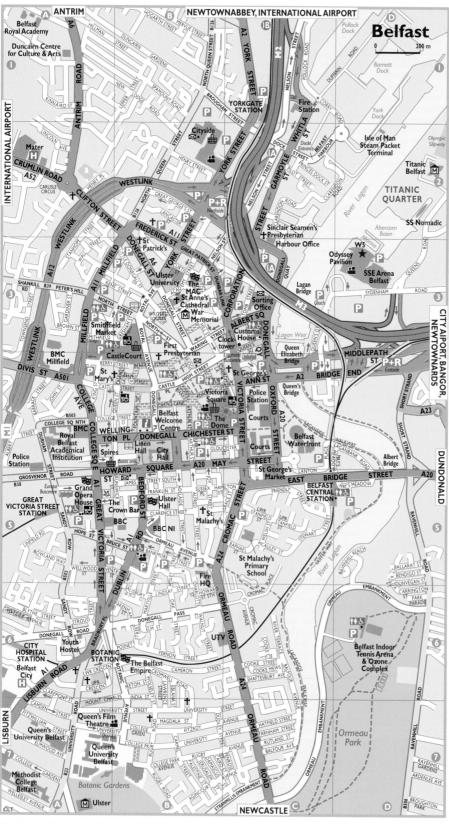

Belfast

TITANIC QUARTER

Corry Road	C1	Penrose Street	C2
Cromac Avenue	C6	Peter's Hill	A3
Cromac Place	C6	Pilot Street	C2
Cromac Street	C5	Pollock Road	C1
Cromwell Road	B6	Posnett Street	B6
Curtis Street	B3	Princes Dock Street	C2
Damascus Street	B7	Queen Elizabeth Bridge	C4
Divis Street	A4	Queen Street	B4
Dock Street	C2	Queen's Bridge	C4
Donegall Pass	B6	Queen's Quay	C3
Donegall Place	B4	Queen's Square	C3
Donegall Quay	C3	Queens Road	D3
Donegall Road	A6	Raphael Street	C5
Donegall Square	B4	Ravenhill Gardens	D7
Donegall Street	B3	Ravenhill Reach	D5
Dublin Road	B6	Ravenhill Road	D5
Dudley Street	B7	River Terrace	C6
Dufferin Road	C1	Rowland Way	A5
Dunbar Link	B3	Royal Avenue	B3
Duncairn Gardens	B1	Rugby Avenue	B7
Dunvegan Street	D5	Rugby Road	B7
Durham Street	A4	Rutland Street	C7
East Bridge Street	C5	St Kilda Street	D5
Eblana Street	B6	Salisbury Street	B6
Elm Street	B6	Sandy Row	A5
Elmwood Avenue	A7	Shaftesbury Avenue	C6
Farnham Street	C7	Shankill Road	A3
Fitzroy Avenue	B7	Short Strand	D4
Fitzwilliam Street	A7	Smithfield	A3
Fountain Street	B4	Spamount Road	B1
Franklin Street	B5	Stanhope Street	A3
Frederick Street	B2	Stewart Street	C5
Friendly Street	C5	Stranmillis Embankment	B7
Gardiner Street	A3	Stroud Street	A6
Garmoyle Street	C2	Sussex Place	B5
Gloucester Street	B4	Sydenham Road	D3
Grace Street	C5	Talbot Street	B3
Great George's Street	B2	Tomb Street	C3
Great Patrick Street	B3	Townsend Street	A3
Great Victoria Street	A5	University Avenue	B7
Gresham Street	B3	University Road	A7
Grosvenor Road	A5	University Square	A7
Hamilton Street	B5	University Street	B7
Hatfield Street	C7	Upper Arthur Street	B4
Henry Place	A2	Upper Crescent	A6
Henry Street	B2	Upper Stanfield Street	C5
High Street	B4	Ventry Street	A5
Hill Street	B3	Vernon Street	B6
Hillman Street	A1	Victoria Street	C4
Hogarth Street	B1	Wall Street	A3
Hope Street	A5	Walnut Street	B6
Howard Street	A5	Waring Street	B3
Howard Street South	B6	Wellesley Avenue	A7
India Street	B6	Wellington Place	A4
Ireton Street	B6	Wellwood Street	A5
James Street South	B5	Welsh Street	C5
Jerusalem Street	B7	Westlink	A3
John Street	A4	Whitla Street	C1
Joy Street	B5	Wolseley Street	B6
Kent Street	A3	Writers' Square	B3
King Street	A4	York Street	B3
Kinnaird Street	A1		
Lagan Bridge	C3		
Laganbank Road	C4		
Lancaster Street	B2		
Lanyon Place	C5		
Lawrence Street	B6		
Lepper Street	B1		
Lincoln Avenue	A2		
Lindsay Street	B6		
Linfield Road	A5		
Lisburn Road	A7		
Little Donegall Street	B3		
Lower Crescent	A6		
Lower Stanfield Street	C5		
Magdala Street	B7		
Maryville Street	B6		
Matilda Avenue	A6		
May Street	B4		
May's Meadow	D5		
McAuley Street	C5		
Mervue Street	B1		
Middlepath Street	D4		
Millfield	A3		
Mount Charles	A7		
Nelson Street	B3		
Nelson Street	C1		
New Lodge Road	B1		
North Queen Street	B2		
North Street	A3		
North Street	B3		
Oak Street	B6		
Ormeau Avenue	B5		
Ormeau Embankment	C7		
Ormeau Road	C6		
Oxford Street	C4		
Pakenham Street	B6		
Palestine Street	B7		
Park Parade	D6		

Belfast is found on atlas page **63 J8**

Academy Street	B3	Bankmore Street	B5	Brunswick Street	B5	Clarendon Road	C2
Adelaide Street	B5	Barrack Street	A4	Cairo Street	B7	Clifton Street	A2
Agincourt Avenue	B7	Bedford Street	B5	Camden Street	A7	College Avenue	A4
Albert Bridge	D4	Belfast Harbour	C2	Cameron Street	B6	College Gardens	A7
Albert Square	C3	Bendigo Street	D5	Carlisle Circus	A2	College Green	B7
Albert Street	A4	Berry Street	A4	Carmel Street	B7	College Park	B7
Alfred Street	B5	Berry Street	B4	Carrington Street	D6	College Park Avenue	B7
Ann Street	B4	Blythe Street	A6	Castle Lane	B4	College Square East	A4
Ann Street	C4	Botanic Avenue	B6	Castle Place	B4	College Square North	A4
Antrim Road	A2	Bradbury Place	A6	Castle Street	A4	College Street	A4
Apsley Street	B6	Bridge End	C4	Chapel Lane	B4	Cooke Court	C6
Ardenlee Avenue	D7	Bridge Street	B4	Charlotte Street	B6	Cooke Mews	C6
Arthur Street	B4	Brougham Street	B1	Chichester Street	B4	Cooke Street	C6
Balfour Avenue	C7	Broughton Park	D7	Church Lane	B4	Cornmarket	B4
Ballarat Street	D5	Brown Street	A3	Claremont Street	A6	Corporation Square	C3
Bank Street	B4	Bruce Street	A5	Clarence Street	B5	Corporation Street	C3

Cork is found on atlas page **6 C4**

8 Street	A4	Friar's Walk	B4
Abbey Street	B4	George's Quay	B4
Academy Street	B3	Gerald Griffin Street	B1
Albert Quay	C3	Gillabbey Street	A4
Albert Road	D3	Glenryan Road	A2
Albert Street	D3	Grand Parade	B3
Albert Street	D3	Grattan Street	A3
Alexandra Road	D1	Green Street	A4
Alfred Street	D2	Greenmount Avenue	A4
Allinett's Lane	B1	Gregg Road	A4
Anderson's Quay	C3	Grenville Place	A2
Anglesea Street	C3	Griffith Bridge	A2
Audley Place	C1	Hanover Street	A3
Bachelor's Quay	A2	Hardwick Street	B2
Ballyhooly Road	D1	Henry Street	A3
Bandon Road	A4	Hibernian Road	C4
Barrack Street	A4	High Street	C4
Beasley Street	B1	Hillgrove Lane	B1
Belgrave Avenue	C2	Horgan's Quay	D2
Bellevue Terrace	D1	Industry Street	B4
Bishop Street	A4	Infirmary Road	C4
Blackpool Bypass	B1	John Redmond Street	B2
Blarney Street	A2	John Street	B2
Bonaventure Place	A4	Kyle Street	B2
Boreenmanna Road	D4	Kyrls Quay	A2
Boyces Street	A2	Kyrls Street	B3
Brian Boru Bridge	C2	Langford Row	C4
Camden Quay	B2	Lapp's Quay	C3
Carey's Lane	B3	Lavitt's Quay	B2
Cat Lane	B4	Leitrim Street	B1
Cathedral Road	A1	Leitrim Street	B2
Cathedral Walk	B1	Liberty Street	A3
Christy Ring Bridge	B2	Lower Glanmire Road	C2
Church Street	B2	Lynchs Street	A3
Clarke's Bridge	A3	MacCurtain Street	C2
Clontarf Bridge	C3	Marina Terrace	D3
Clontarf Street	C3	Marlboro Street	B3
Coach Street	A3	Mary Aitkenhead Place	A2
Coal Quay	B2	Mary Street	B4
Cook Street	B3	Maylor Street	C3
Copley Street	C4	Merchant's Quay	C2
Cornmarket Street	B3	Michael Collins Bridge	D3
Cotter Street	C4	Military Hill	D1
Cove Street	B4	Morgan Street	C3
Crosses Green Quay	A3	Morrison's Quay	C3
Dean Street	A4	Mount Carmel Road	B4
Dominick Street	B2	Mount Sion Road	A4
Douglas Street	C4	Nicholas Street	B4
Drinan Street	B4	Noonan Road	A4
Eamon de Valera Bridge	D3	North Main Street	A2
East View Terrace	C4	North Mall	A2
Eglinton Street	C3	North Monastery Road	A1
Evergreen Street	B4	Old Blackrock Road	C4
Fair Street	A2	Old Station Road	C4
Father Mathew Quay	B3	Old Youghal Road	C1
Father Mathew Street	B3	Oliver Plunkett Street	B3
Fitton Street East	C3	Oliver Plunkett Street Lower	C3
Fort Street	A4	Opera Lane	B3
Francis Street	B4	Parkowen	C4
French's Quay	A3	Parliament Bridge	B3
French's Villas	A1	Parnell Bridge	C3
Friar's Street	B4	Parnell Place	C3

Paul Street	B3	Robert Street	B3	Sharman Crawford Street	A4	Townsend Place	B4
Penrose Quay	C2	Rockboro Avenue	D4	Sheare Street	A3	Trinity Bridge	C4
Peter's Street	A3	Rockboro Road	D4	Ship Street	D2	Tuckey Street	B3
Pine Street	B2	Roman Street	B1	Sidney Park	C2	Union Quay	C3
Pope's Hill	B1	Rutland Street	C4	Smith Street	C3	Upper John Street	B1
Pope's Quay	B2	St Finnbarre's Bridge	A3	South Gate Bridge	B3	Vicar Street	A4
Pope's Road	B1	St Kevin's Street	B4	South Link Road	D3	Victoria Road	D3
Presentation Place	B4	St Mary's Road	B1	South Main Street	B3	Wandesford Quay	A3
Princes' Street	B3	St Patrick Street	B3	South Mall	B3	Washington Street	A3
Quaker Road	C4	St Patrick's Bridge	C2	South Terrace	C4	Watercourse Road	B1
Railway Street	D2	St Patrick's Hill	C2	Southern Road	C4	Wellington Road	C2
Rathmore Park	B1	St Patrick's Quay	C2	Sullivan's Quay	B3	White Street	C4
Rathmore Road	D1	St Paul's Avenue	B2	Summerhill North	D2	Winthrop Street	C3
Redemption Road	B1	St Vincent's Street	A1	Summerhill South	C4	Wolfe Tone Street	A1
Reeds Square	B4	Sawmill Street	C4	Sunvalley Drive	A1	Woods Street	A3
Richmond Hill	B1	Shandon Street	A2	Tower Street	B4	York Street	C2

Galway is found on atlas page **34 B8**

Abbeygate Street	B2	Gaol Road	B2	Raleigh Row	A3
Ashgrove Road	A2	Headford Road	C1	St Augustine Street	B3
Beggars Bridge	A2	Henry Street	A3	St Brendan's Avenue	B2
Bohermore	C1	High Street	B3	St Bridget's Place	C1
Bóthar Brendan Ui Heithir	C2	Lombard Street	B2	St Enda's Road	A2
Bóthar Irwin	C2	Lough Atalia Road	C3	St Francis Street	B2
Bóthar na Dige	B1	Lower Canal Road	A2	St Helens Street	A3
Bóthar na Long	C3	Lower Dominick Street	B3	St Mary's Road	A3
Bóthar na Mban	C1	Lower Fairhill Road	B3	St Patrick's Avenue	C2
Bowling Green	B2	Lower Newcastle Road	A1	St Vincent's Avenue	B2
Bridge Street	B3	Market Street	B2	Salmon Weir Bridge	B2
Canal Walk	A3	Mary Street	B2	Sea Road	A3
Cill Ard	C1	Merchants Street	C3	Shantalla Road	A2
Claddagh Quay	B3	Middle Street	B3	Spanish Parade	B3
Costello Road	A2	Munster Avenue	A3	Station Road	C2
Cross Street	B3	New Road	A3	The Long Walk	B3
Dock Road	C3	New Street West	A3	The Plots Road	B1
Dock Street	C3	Newcastle Avenue	A1	University Road	A1
Dyke Road	B1	Newcastle Park	A1	Upper Canal Road	A2
Earl's Island	B2	Newtownsmith	B2	Victoria Place	C2
Eglinton Street	B2	Nun's Island	B2	Walsh's Terrace	B2
Eyre Square	C2	O'Briens Bridge	B3	Waterlane	C1
Eyre Square East	C2	Palmyra Avenue	A3	Waterside	B2
Eyre Street	C2	Palmyra Park	A3	William Street	B2
Father Griffin Road	B3	Parkavara	A3	Willow Park	A2
Flood Street	B3	Presentation Road	A2	Wolfe Tone Bridge	B3
Forster Court	C2	Prospect Hill	C2	Wood Quay	B2
Forster Street	C2	Queen Street	C3		

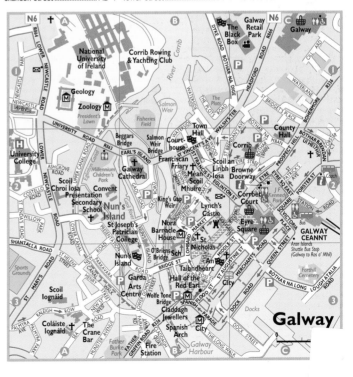

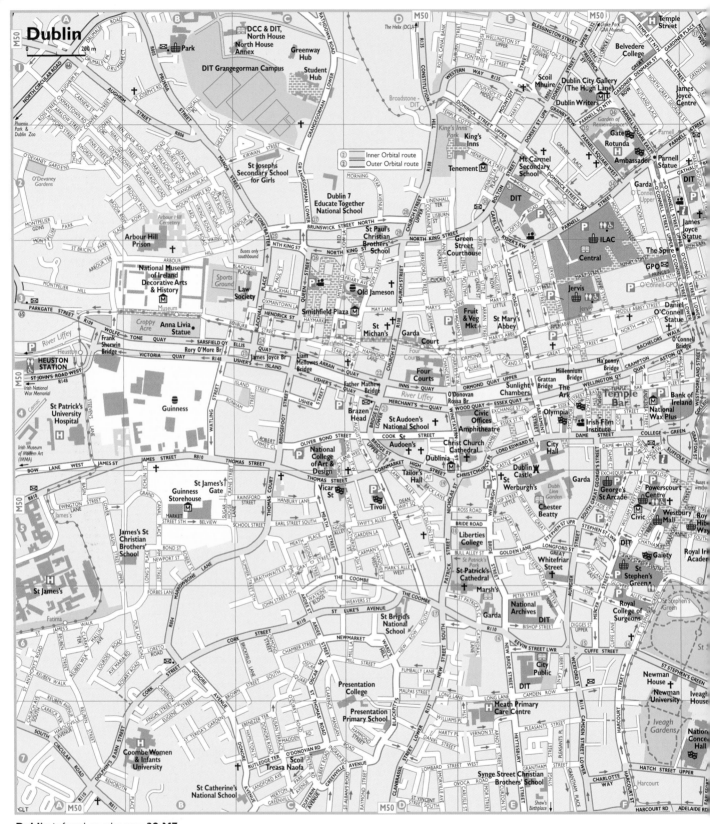

Dublin is found on atlas page **39 M7**

Abbey Street Lower G3	Aughrim Place A1	Blessington Street E1	Burgh Quay G3	Chatham Street F5	Cope Street F4	Denzille Lane ....
Adelaide Road F7	Aughrim Street A1	Bolton Street E2	Butt Bridge G3	Chimney View K5	Cork Street B6	Digges Lane ....
Admiral Brown Street K4	Aungier Street F6	Bond Street B5	Byrne's Lane J4	Christchurch Place E5	Cornmarket D5	Digges Street Upper ....
Amiens Street H2	Ave Maria Road A6	Bonham Street B4	Camden Row E6	Church Avenue South A7	Cowper Street A2	Dolphin's Barn Road ....
Anglesea Row E3	Bachelors Walk F3	Bow Lane East F5	Camden Street Lower F7	Church Road K1	Crampton Quay F4	Dominick Street Lower ......
Anglesea Street F4	Back Lane D5	Bow Lane West A5	Cameron Street B6	Church Road K2	Crane Street B5	Dominick Street Upper ......
Anne Street North D3	Baggot Lane K7	Bow Street D3	Canon Lillis Avenue J2	Church Street D3	Creighton Street J4	Donore Avenue ....
Anne Street South F5	Baggot Street Lower H6	Boyne Street H5	Capel Road E2	Church Street Upper D2	Crinan Strand J2	Donore Road ....
Arbour Hill B3	Barrow Street K6	Braithwaite St C5	Capel Street E2	City Quay H3	Cuckoo Lane D3	Dorset Street Upper ....
Arbour Place C2	Basin Street Lower A5	Bride Road D5	Cardiff Lane K4	Clanbrassil Street Lower D7	Cuffe Lane F6	Drumalee Court ....
Arbour Terrace A3	Basin Street Upper A5	Bride Street E5	Carlisle Street E7	Clanwilliam Place K6	Cuffe Street F6	Drumalee Park ....
Ard Righ Road B2	Beaver Street H2	Bridge Street Lower D4	Carman's Hall D5	Clare Street H5	Cumberland Road H7	Drumalee Road ....
Ardee Street C6	Bella Street H1	Bridge Street Upper D4	Carnew Street A1	Clarence Mangan Road C6	Cumberland Street North G2	Drury Street ....
Arklow Street A1	Belview B5	Bridgefoot Street C4	Carrick Terrace A7	Clarence Place Great J5	Curzon Street E7	Dufferin Avenue ....
Arnott Street E7	Ben Edair Road A2	Brodir Row A2	Cathal Brugha Street G2	Clarendon Street F5	Custom House Harbour H2	Duke Lane ....
Arran Quay C4	Benburb Street B3	Brown Street D3	Cathedral Lane E6	Clarke's Terrace A6	Custom House Quay H3	Dunne Street ....
Arran Street East E3	Beresford Place H3	Brown Street South B6	Catherine Street D5	College Green F4	D'Olier Street G4	Earl Street South ....
Asgard Road K4	Beresford Street D3	Brunswick Place J5	Chamber Street C6	College Street G4	Dame Court F4	Earlsfort Terrace ....
Ash Street D5	Bishop Street E6	Brunswick Street North C2	Chancery Lane E5	Commons Street J3	Dame Lane F4	Eastmoreland Lane ....
Ashford Street A1	Blackhall Parade C3	Buckingham Street Lower .. H1	Chancery Place D4	Constitution Hill D1	Dame Street F4	Ebenezer Terrace ....
Aston Place F4	Blackhall Place C3	Buckingham Street Upper .. H1	Charles Street West D4	Cook Street D4	Daniel Street D7	Eblana Villas ....
Aston Quay F4	Blackhall Street C3	Bull Alley Street D5	Charlotte Way F7	Coburg Place J2	Dawson Street G5	Echlin Street ....
Auburn Street E1	Blackpitts D7				Dean Swift Square D5	Eden Quay ....

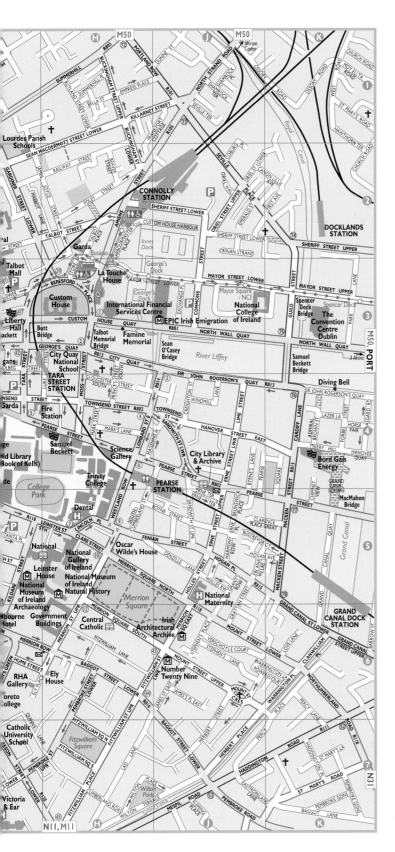

Harbourmaster Place........H2
Harcourt Road........F7
Harcourt Street........F7
Hardwicke Street........FI
Harmony Row........J5
Harold Road........B2
Haroldville Avenue........A7
Harty Place........D7
Hatch Street Lower........G7
Hatch Street Upper........G7
Hawkins Street........G3
Hawthorn Terrace........KI
Haymarket........C3
Hendrick Street........C3
Henrietta Place........E2
Henrietta Street........E2
Henry Street........F3
Herbert Place........J7
Herbert Street........J7
Heytesbury Street........E7
High Street........D4
Hill Street........FI
Hogan Avenue........J5
Hogan Place........J5
Holles Row........J5
Holles Street........J5
Horse Fair........K4
Hume Street........G6
Ingram Road........C7
Inns Quay........D4
Island Street........C4
Ivar Street........B2
James Joyce Bridge........C4
James Joyce Street........G2
James Street........B4
James Street East........J6
James's Place East........J6
Jervis Street........E3
John Dillon Street........D5
John Street South........C6
John Street West........C5
John's Lane West........C5
Kevin Street Lower........E6
Kildare Street........G5
Killarney Street........HI
King Street South........F5
King's Inn's Street........E2
Kirwan Street........C2
Lad Lane........H7
Lamb Alley........D5
Lazer Lane........K4
Leeson Street Lower........G7
Leinster Street South........G5
Liam Mellows Bridge........C4
Liberty Lane........E6
Liffey Street........F3
Lime Street........J4
Lincoln Lane........D4
Lincoln Place........H5
Linenhall Terrace........D2
Lisburn Street........D2
Little Britain Street........E3
Little Green Street........D3
Little Strand Street........E4
Loftus Road........CI
Lombard Street East........H4
Lombard Street West........D7
Long Lane........D6
Long's Place........B5
Longford Street Great........E5
Lord Edward Street........E4
Loreto Road........A6
Lourdes Road........A6
Love Lane........K6
Luke Street........H4
Mabbot Lane........G2
Macken Street........K5
Macmahon Bridge........K5
Madden Road........C7
Magennis Place........H4
Malachi Road........B2
Mallin Avenue........A6
Malpas Street........D6
Manor Place........B2
Manor Street........B2
Market Street South........B5
Mark's Alley West........D5
Mark's Lane........H4
Mark Street........H4
Marlborough Street........G2
Marrowbone Lane........B6
Mary's Abbey........E3
Mary's Lane........D3
Mary Street........E3
Mary Street Little........E3
May Lane........D3
Mayor Street Lower........H3
Mayor Street Lower........J3
Meath Place........C5
Meath Street........C5
Mercer Street........F6
Merchant's Quay........D4
Merrion Row........G6
Merrion Square East........J6
Merrion Square North........H5
Merrion Square South........H6
Merrion Street Upper........H6
Merton Park........C7
Mespil Road........J7

Murtagh Road........B2
Nassau Street........G5
New Bride Street........E6
New Row South........D6
New Street South........D6
Newmarket........C6
Newport Street........B5
Niall Street........A2
Nicholas Street........D5
Norseman Place........B2
North Circular Road........AI
North Earl Street........G3
North Frederick Street........FI
North Great George's Street........FI
North King Street........C3
North Lotts........F3
North Strand Road........JI
North Wall Quay........J3
Northumberland Road........K6
O'Connell Bridge........G3
O'Connell Street Lower........F3
O'Connell Street Upper........F2
O'Curry Road........C6
O'Devaney Gardens........A2
O'Donovan Road........C7
O'Donovan Rossa Bridge........D4
Olaf Road........B2
Oliver Bond Street........C4
Ormond Quay Upper........E4
Ormond Square........E4
Ormond Street........C6
Oscar Square........C6
Ossory Road........JI
Ostan Place........B2
Our Lady's Road........B6
Ovoca Road........D7
Oxmantown Lane........C3
Oxmantown Road........AI
Park Lane........K3
Parkgate Street........A3
Parliament Street........E4
Parnell Square East........FI
Parnell Square North........F2
Parnell Square West........F2
Parnell Street........F2
Patrick Street........D5
Paul Street........C3
Pearse Square........J4
Pearse Street........H4
Pembroke Gardens........K7
Pembroke Road........J7
Pembroke Street Lower........H6
Pembroke Street Upper........G7
Percy Lane........K6
Percy Place........J7
Peter Street........E6
Peter's Row........E6
Petrie Road........C7
Pim Street........B5
Pimlico........C5
Pleasants Place........E7
Pleasants Street........E7
Poolbeg Street........G3
Portland Row........HI
Powerscourt........J6
Price's Lane........F4
Primrose Street........EI
Prince's Street North........F3
Prince's Street South........H4
Provost Row........B2
Prussia Street........BI
Queen Street........C3
Quinn's Lane........G6
Railway Street........H2
Rainsford Street........C5
Rathdown Road........CI
Raymond Street........D7
Red Cow Lane........D3
Reginald Street........C5
Rehoboth Place........A7
Reuben Avenue........A6
Reuben Street........A6
Reuben Walk........A6
Robert Emmet Close........C4
Robert Street........B5
Rory O'More Bridge........B3
Rosary Road........A6
Rosie Hackett Bridge........G3
Ross Road........E5
Ross Street........AI
Rostrevor Court........J5
Royal Canal Bank........DI
Rutland Place........FI
Rutland Street Lower........HI
Rutledge Terrace........C7
Ryder's Row........E2
Sackville Place........G3
St Alban's Road........D7
St Andrew Street........F4
St Anthony's Road........A6
St Augustine Street........D4
St Bricin's Park........A3
St James's Walk........A6
St John's Road West........A4
St Joseph's Road........BI
St Luke's Avenue........C6
St Mary's Lane........K7
St Mary's Road........KI
St Mary's Road........K7
St Mary's Terrace........EI
St Michan's Street........D3
St Patrick's Close........E6
St Stephen's Green........F6
St Teresa's Gardens........B7
St Thomas' Road........C6
St Vincent Street South........D7
Samuel Beckett Bridge........K3
Sandford Avenue........C7
Sandwith Street Lower........J4
Sandwith Street Upper........J5
Sarsfield Quay........B3
School Street........B5
Sean MacDermott Street
    Lower........G2
Sean O'Casey Bridge........J3
Setanta Place........G5
Seville Place........J2
Seville Terrace........JI
Shamrock Place........JI

Shamrock Terrace........JI
Shea's Lane........B2
Sheriff Street Lower........J2
Sheriff Street Upper........K2
Ship Street Great........E5
Ship Street Little........E5
Sigurd Road........B2
Sir John Rogerson's Quay........J4
Sitric Road........B2
Slade Row........A2
Smithfield........C3
South Circular Road........A7
South Cumberland Street........H5
South Frederick Street........G5
Spencer Dock Bridge........K3
Stable Lane........C3
Steeven's Lane........A4
Stephen Street Lower........F5
Stephen Street Upper........E5
Stephen's Lane........J6
Stephen's Place........J6
Stoneybatter........C2
Store Street........H3
Suffolk Street........F4
Sugar House Lane........B5
Summer Street South........C5
Summerhill........HI
Summerhill Place........HI
Susan Terrace........C7
Swift's Alley........D5
Swords Street........A2
Sycamore Street........F4
Synge Street........E7
Talbot Memorial Bridge........H3
Talbot Place........H2
Talbot Street........H2
Tara Street........G4
Temple Bar........F4
Temple Cotts........DI
Temple Lane North........GI
Temple Lane South........F4
Temple Street North........FI
The Coombe........C5
Thomas Court........C5
Thomas Street........C5
Thor Place........A2
Townsend Street........G4
Trinity Street........F4
Upper Abbey Street........E3
Usher Street........C4
Usher's Island........C4
Usher's Quay........C4
Vernon Street........E7
Verschoyle Court........J6
Vicar Street........D5
Victoria Quay........B4
Viking Place........B3
Viking Road........B2
Ward's Hill........D6
Warrington Lane........J6
Warrington Place........K6
Watkins Buildings........C6
Watling Street........B4
Weavers Street........D6
Wellington Quay........F4
Wellington Street Lower........EI
Wellington Street Upper........EI
Wentworth Place........E5
West Road........KI
Western Way........DI
Westland Row........H5
Westmoreland Street........G4
Wexford Street........F6
Whitefriar Street........E5
Wicklow Street........F5
William Street South........F5
Williams Place South........D7
Wilton Place........H7
Wilton Terrace........H7
Windmill Lane........J4
Winetavern Street........D4
Wolfe Tone Quay........A3
Wolfe Tone Street........E3
Wood Quay........E4
York Street........F6

lis Quay........C3
y Place........G6
merald Street........J2
nor Street........E7
norville Avenue........D7
mpress Place........HI
ngine Alley........C5
ne Place........J5
ne Street Lower........J4
ne Street Upper........J5
ne Terrace........J5
ssex Quay........E4
ssex Street East........E4
ssex Street West........E4
ugene Street........B7
xington Lane........A5
xchange Place........J3
xchange Street Lower........E4
xchequer Street........F5
ade Street........F5
ather Mathew Bridge........D4
enian Street........H5

Fingal Street........B7
Fingall Place........BI
Finn Street........A2
First Avenue........K2
Fishamble Street........E4
Fitzwilliam Lane........H6
Fitzwilliam Place........H7
Fitzwilliam Square North........H7
Fitzwilliam Square South........H7
Fitzwilliam Street Lower........H6
Fitzwilliam Street Upper........H7
Fleet Street........F4
Fleming Place........J7
Foley Street........H2
Fontenoy Street........EI
Forbes Lane........B6
Forbes Street........K4
Francis Street........D5
Frankfort Cottage........HI
Frank Sherwin Bridge........A3
Friary Avenue........D3
Fumbally Lane........D6
Garden Lane........D5

Gardiner Place........FI
Gardiner Row........FI
Gardiner Street Lower........G2
Gardiner Street Middle........GI
George's Hill........D3
George's Quay........G3
Gilbert Road........C7
Gloucester Street South........H4
Glovers Alley........F5
Godfrey Place........A2
Golden Lane........E5
Grafton Street........F5
Grafton Street........G4
Granby Place........E2
Granby Row........EI
Grand Canal Place........B5
Grand Canal Quay........K6
Grand Canal Square........K4
Grand Canal Street Lower........K5
Grand Canal Street Upper........K6
Grangegorman Lower........C2
Grant's Row........J5
Grantham Place........E7

Grantham Street........E7
Grattan Bridge........E4
Grattan Street........J6
Gray Street........C5
Great Denmark Street........FI
Great Strand Street........E3
Greek Street........D3
Green Street........E3
Greenville Avenue........C7
Grenville Street........GI
Guild Street........K3
Ha'penny Bridge........F4
Haddington Place........K7
Haddington Road........J7
Halliday Road........B2
Halston Street........D3
Hamilton Street........B6
Hammond Lane........D3
Hammond Street........D7
Hanbury Lane........C5
Hanover Quay........K4
Hanover Street East........J4
Hanover Street West........D5

Kilkenny is found on atlas page 21 N3

Abbey Street	A2	Gaol Road	A3	New Road	B1
Back Lane	B2	Golf Links Road	C1	Newpark Drive	B1
Ballybought Street	C1	Granges Road	A1	O'Loughlin Road	C2
Barrack Street	B2	Green Street	A1	Ormonde Road	B3
Bateman's Quay	B2	Green's Bridge	A1	Ormonde Street	A1
Bishop's Hill	A1	Greens Hill	B1	Ossory Park	C1
Black Mill Street	A2	Greensbridge Street	B1	Parliament Street	A2
Broguemakers Hill	B1	Haughney Green	A3	Parnell Street	A3
Butts Green	A2	Hebron Road	C1	Patrick Street	B2
Canal Square	B3	High Street	A2	Riverside Drive	A1
Canal Walk	C3	Irishtown	A2	Rose Inn Street	B3
Castle Gardens	B3	James's Street	A2	St Francis Bridge	B1
Castle Road	B3	John Street Lower	B2	St Kieran's Street	B2
Castlecomer Road	B1	John Street Upper	B2	St Maul's	B1
Church Lane	A1	John's Bridge	B3	St Rioch's Street	A3
Coach Road	A2	John's Quay	B2	Stephen's Street	A3
De Loughry Place	A2	Kickham Street	A3	The Parade	B3
Dean Street	A2	Lacken Drive	C2	The Ring	A2
Dominic Street	A3	Lakeview Drive	C1	Thomas Street	A2
Dublin Road	C2	Lintown Avenue	C1	Troy's Gate	A1
Evan's Lane	A2	Lower New Street	A3	Troy's Lane	A1
Father Hayden Road	B3	Market Yard	A2	Vicar Street	A1
Freshford Road	A1	Maudlin Street	B2	Walkin Street	A3
Friars Bridge	A2	Michael Street	B2	William Street	A3
Friary Street	A3	New Building Lane	A2	Wolfe Tone Street	B2

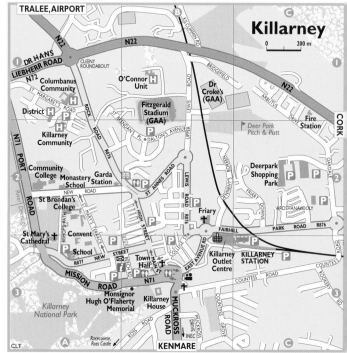

Killarney is found on atlas page 10 B6

Arbutus Drive	C1	Fairhill	B2	Park Road	C2
Ardshanavooly	C2	Friary Downs	C2	Port Road	A2
Beech Road	B3	High Street	B2	Rock Road	A1
Bishop's Path	A3	Kilcummin Road	B1	Rookery Road	C3
Bridgefield	B1	Lewis Road	B2	Ross Road	B3
College Street	B3	Main Street	B3	St Annes Road	B2
Countess Grove	B3	Mission Road	A3	St Brendan's Place	A1
Countess Road	C3	Muckross Drive	B3	St Margaret's Road	A1
Dalton's Avenue	B2	Muckross Road	B3	St Mary's Terrace	A2
Dennehy's Boreen	B2	New Road	A2	Upper Lewis Road	B2
Dr Hans Liebherr Road	A1	New Street	A3		
East Avenue Road	B3	Oakdale	C2		

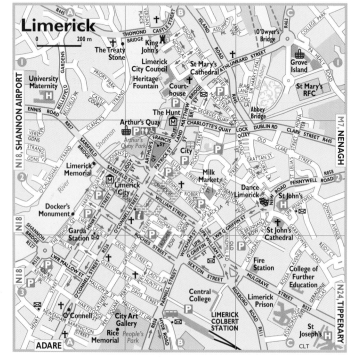

Limerick is found on atlas page 18 H3

Abbey Bridge	C1	Barrington Street	A3	Broad Street	B2
Abbey View	B1	Bedford Row	A2	Carr Street	B2
Arthur's Quay	B2	Bellefield Gardens	A1	Castle Street	B1
Assumpta Park	B1	Bellfield Park	A1	Cathedral Place	C3
Athlunkard Street	B1	Bishops Street	B1	Catherine Place	A3
Baal's Bridge	B1	Brennan's Row	C2	Catherine Street	A3
Back Lane	B2	Bridge Street	B1	Cecil Street	A3

Charlotte's Quay	B2	John Street	C2	Pery Street	A3
Clancy's Strand	A2	Lady's Lane	B3	Priory Park	A1
Clare Street	C2	Liddy Street	B2	Reidy Court	C3
College Park	C1	Lock Quay	C2	Robert Street	B2
Court Castle	A1	Long Lane	C1	Roches Row	B3
Cruise's Street	B2	Lower Cecil Street	A2	Roches Street	B3
Curry Lane	C2	Lower Gerald Griffin		Rossa Avenue	C3
Davis Street	B3	Street	B3	Roxboro Road	C3
Denmark Street	B2	Lower Mallow Street	A3	Roxborough Avenue	C3
Downey Avenue	C2	Mallow Street	A3	Rutland Street	B2
Dublin Road	C2	Mallow Street Upper	A3	St Lelia's Street	C2
Ellen Street	B2	Mary Street	B1	Sarsfield Bridge	A2
Ennis Road	A1	Matthew Bridge	B1	Sarsfield Street	A2
Flag Lane	C1	Michael Street	B2	Sean Heuston Place	B2
Foxe's Bow	B2	Mill Lane	A3	Sexton Street	B3
Francis Street	B2	Mona Terrace	C2	Shannon Bridge	A2
Gaol Lane	B1	Mount Kennett Place	A3	Sheep Street	B1
Garryowen Road	C2	Mulgrave Street	C3	Sir Harry's Mall	C1
Georges Quay	B1	Mungret Street	B2	Strandville Gardens	A2
Geraldine Villas	C3	New Road	C2	Summer Street	C2
Glentworth Street	A3	Newenham Street	A3	The Bishop's Quay	A2
Grattan Street	C2	Nicholas Street	B1	Thomas Street	B2
Hartstonge Street	A3	O'Callaghan Strand	A2	Thomond Bridge	A1
Harvey's Quay	A2	O'Connell Street	A3	Upper Gerald Griffin	
Henry Street	A2	O'Dwyer's Bridge	C1	Street	B2
Henry Street	A3	Old Clare Street	C2	Upper Pennywell	C2
High Street	B2	Old Windmill Road	B3	Upper William Street	B2
Honan's Quay	A2	Pa Healy Road	B3	Verdant Place	B1
Hunts Lane	B3	Parnell Street	B3	Vereker Gardens	A2
Hyde Road	B3	Patrick Street	B2	Wickham Street	B3
Island Road	B1	Pennywell Road	C2	William Street	B2
James Street	C2	Pery Square	A3		

Londonderry Derry is found on atlas page 66 C9

...bey Street................A1	Foyle Road................B3	Nailors Road................A2
...bots Walk................A2	Foyle Street................B2	Oakfield Road................A1
...ercorn Road................B3	Foyleside................C3	Orchard Street................B2
...rrack Street................A3	Francis Street................A1	Palace Street................B2
...echwood Avenue................A1	Frederick Street................A1	Patrick Street................B1
...hop Street Within................B2	Great James Street................A1	Peace Bridge................C1
...hop Street Without................A3	Harbour Square................B1	Princes Street................B2
...dge Street................B2	Harvey Street................B2	Pump Street................B2
...owning Drive................C1	Hawkin Street................B2	Queen Street................B1
...tcher Street................A2	High Street................B2	Queen's Quay................B1
...bel Street................A2	Infirmary Road................A1	Railway Road................C3
...rlisle Road................B3	Ivy Terrace................B3	Rossville Street................B2
...stle Street................B2	John Street................B3	Stanley's Walk................A2
...amberlain Street................B2	Kennedy Street................B3	Strand Road................B1
...arendon Street................B1	Lecky Road................A2	The Diamond................B2
...aigavon Bridge................C3	Lecky Road................A3	The Fountain................B2
...eggan Road................A1	Limewood Street................A2	Upper Bennett Street................B3
...eggan Street................A1	Linenhall Street................B2	Wapping Lane................B3
...ve Gardens................A2	Little James Street................B1	Water Street................C2
...ke Street................C3	London Street................B2	Waterloo Place................B1
...ncliffe Avenue................A2	Lone Moor Road................A2	Waterside Link................C2
...nwood Road................A2	Magazine Street................B2	Westland Avenue................A1
...han Street................A1	Market Street................B2	Westland Street................A2
...han Street................B2	Marlborough Avenue................A1	Westland Terrace................A2
...rguson Street................A3	Marlborough Street................A1	William Street................A1
...rryquay Street................B2	Mary Street................A3	William Street................B1
...yle Embankment................C2	Miller Street................A3	

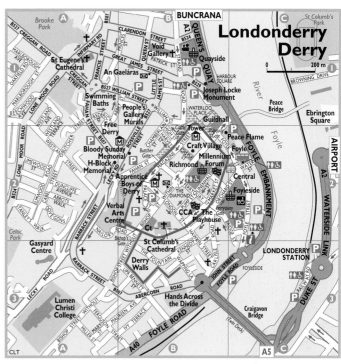

Sligo is found on atlas page 52 C5

Abbey Street................C2	Holborn Hill................B1	Pearse Road................C3
Abbey Street Lower................C2	Holborn Street................B1	Pim Mill Road................A1
Adelaide Street................A2	Hughes Bridge................B1	Quay Street................B1
Ballast Quay................A1	Hyde Bridge................B2	Rathedmond................A1
Barrack Street................B1	J F Kennedy Parade................C2	Ray McSharry Road................A3
Bridge Street................C2	Jink's Avenue................A2	Riverside................C2
Burton Street................C2	Joe Banks Road................A2	Rockwood Parade................B2
Calry Lane................C1	Joe McDonnell Drive................C3	St Annes Terrace................C2
Castle Street................B2	John Street................C2	St Brigid's Place................C3
Chapel Hill................C2	Kempton Promenade................C2	St Josephs Terrace................B3
Chapel Street................C2	Knappagh Road................A2	Sean Fallon Bridge................C2
Charles Street................B2	Lake Isle Road................C1	Stephen Street................B1
Church Street................B2	Lord Edward Street................B2	Summerhill Roundabout................A3
Circular Road................B3	Lower Knox Street................B2	Summerhill Village................B3
City View................C1	Lower Quay Street................B1	Teeling Street................C2
Citygate................B3	Lynns Dock................A1	Temple Street................B2
Connaughton Road................C1	Magheraboy Road................A3	The Lungy................B2
Connolly Street................B3	Mail Coach Road................B3	The Mall................C1
Cranmore Road................C2	Market Street................B2	Thomas Street................C2
Custom House Quay................B1	Markievicz Road................B1	Union Street................A1
Dominic Street................B3	Michael Conlon Road................A2	Upper John Street................A2
Finiskiln Road................A1	Norbert Ferguson Parade................B2	Water Lane................B2
Gallows Hill................B3	New Street................B1	West Gardens................B2
Grattan Street................B2	O'Connell Street................B2	Wine Street................B2
Harmony Hill................B2	Old Market Street................B2	Wolfe Tone Street................A2
High Street................B2	Old Pound Street................C3	

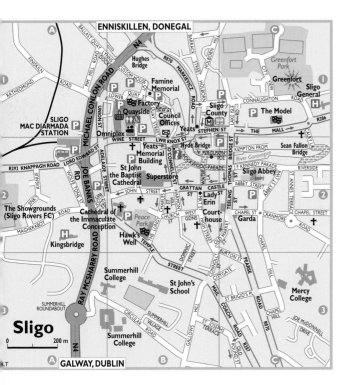

Waterford is found on atlas page 14 E6

...bbey Road................C1	Gracedieu Road................A1	Ozanam Street................A2
...rmount Villas................A2	Grattan Quay................A1	Park Road................C3
...ne Street................A1	Green Street................B2	Parnell Street................B2
...d Na Greine................A3	Griffith Place................A2	Passage Road................C3
...llybricken................A2	Hennessy's Road................A3	Patrick Street................B2
...llytruckle Road................A3	John Street................B2	Penrose Lane................A1
...rrack Street................A3	John Street................B2	Philip Street................A2
...ch Street................B3	Johns Hill................C3	Poleberry Street................B3
...rnard Place................A3	Johnstown................B2	Roanmore Park................A3
...akes Lane................A3	Lady Lane................B2	Rockfield Park................A2
...dge Street................A1	Lower Newtown Road................C3	Ross Road................C1
...nkers Hill................A2	Lower Yellow Road................A2	St Alphonsus Road................C3
...nnon Street................A2	Luke Wadding Street................A2	Slievekeale Road................A3
...stle Street................B2	Manor Street................B3	South Parade................C3
...therine Street................C2	Mary Street................A1	Stephen's Street................B2
...eannt Road................A3	Mayor's Walk................B2	Summerhill................A2
...ty Square................B2	Meagher's Quay................B1	The Glen................A1
...al Quay................B1	Merchant's Quay................A1	The Glen................A2
...ollege Street................B3	Military Road................A2	The Mall................C2
...onnolly Place................A2	Morgan Street................A2	Thomas Hill................B1
...rk Road................B3	Morrison's Road................A2	Thomas Street................A2
...stom House Parade................C2	Morrissons Avenue................A2	Tramore Road................B3
...ock Road................B1	Mount Sion Avenue................B2	Upper Yellow Road................A2
...oyle's Lane................A2	New Street................B2	Water Street................B2
...nmore Road................C2	Newport's Square................A2	Waterside................B2
...mund Rice Bridge................B1	Newtown Road................C3	Wilkin's Street................C3
...untain Street................C1	O'Connell Street................B1	William Street................C2
...ancis Street................B2	Otteran Place................C3	

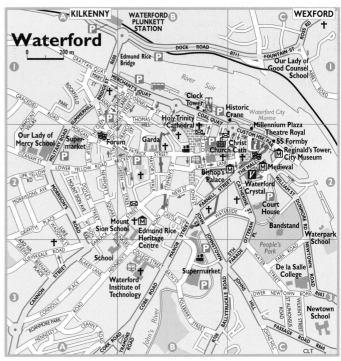

The motorway maps on these pages consist of signposting panels, the layout of junctions, road numbers and exit destinations. To reflect the distances shown on the motorway signs, distances are given in miles in Northern Ireland and in kilometres in the Republic of Ireland.

Northern Ireland

M1	Belfast – Craigavon	80
M1	Craigavon – Dungannon	81
M2	Ballymena Bypass	81
M2, M22	Belfast – Randalstown	80

Republic of Ireland

M1	M50 – Dundalk	82
M2	Kilshane Cross – Ashbourne	83
M3	Clonee – Kells	83
M4	Leixlip – McNead's Bridge	88

M6	M4 – Galway	84
M7	Naas – Limerick	85
M8	M7 – Cork	86
M9	M7 – Waterford	88
M11	Dublin – Gorey	87
M17, M18	Shannon – Tuam	89
M20	Limerick – N21	89
M50	Dublin Ring Road and Port Tunnel	81

Toll motorways

Generally toll charges can be paid at the barrier on the toll road, either in cash or by using an electronic tagging system.

On the M50 Dublin, a barrier-free tolling system operates called **eFlow**. Your number plate will be recorded when you pass through the toll and the fee must be paid by 8pm the following day at the latest. Cash cannot be paid at the toll but the fee can be paid at any 'payzone' outlet or online. For further information see *www.eflow.ie*

Key to motorway maps

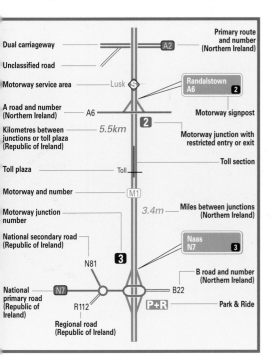

Restricted motorway junctions

Northern Ireland

M1 BELFAST – DUNGANNON

Junction		
3	Westbound	No access, exit only.
	Eastbound	No exit, access only.
7	Westbound	No access, exit only.
	Eastbound	No restriction.

M2, M22 BELFAST – RANDALSTOWN

Junction		
1B	Southbound	No access, exit only.
2	Westbound	No restriction.
	Eastbound	No exit to M5.

Republic of Ireland

M1, M50 – DUNDALK

Junction		
3	Northbound	No access, exit only.
	Southbound	No exit, access only.
8	Northbound	No access, exit only.
	Southbound	No exit, access only.
9	Northbound	No restriction.
	Southbound	No access, exit only.
11	Northbound	No exit, access only.
	Southbound	No access, exit only.
13	Northbound	No access, exit only.
	Southbound	No exit, access only.

M4 LEIXLIP – McNEAD'S BRIDGE

Junction		
10	Westbound	No access, exit only.
	Eastbound	No exit, access only.
11	Westbound	No access, exit only to M6 westbound.
	Eastbound	No exit. No access to M6.
12	Westbound	No exit, access only.
	Eastbound	No access, exit only.

M6, M4 – GALWAY

Junction		
1	Westbound	Exit only to M4 westbound.
	Eastbound	Access only from M4 eastbound.

M7 NAAS – LIMERICK

Junction		
11	Westbound	Exit only to M9 southbound.
	Eastbound	Access only from M9 northbound.
19	Westbound	Exit only to M8 southbound.
	Eastbound	Access only from M8 northbound.
30	Westbound	Exit only to M20 southbound and N18 westbound.
	Eastbound	No restriction.

M8, M7 – CORK

Junction		
1	Northbound	Exit only to M7 eastbound.
	Southbound	Access only from M7 westbound.
5	Northbound	No access, exit only.
	Southbound	No access, exit only.
16	Northbound	No access, exit only.
	Southbound	No exit, access only.

M9, M7 – WATERFORD

Junction		
1	Northbound	Exit only to M7 eastbound.

M11 DUBLIN – GOREY

Junction		
15	Northbound	No exit, access only.
	Southbound	No access, exit only.

M20 LIMERICK – N21

Junction		
1	Northbound	Exit only to N18 & M7.
	Southbound	No restriction.

M50 DUBLIN RING ROAD AND PORT TUNNEL

Junction		
2	Northbound	No exit, access only.
	Southbound	No access, exit only.
13	Northbound	No access, exit only.
	Southbound	No access, exit only.
14	Northbound	No exit, access only.
	Southbound	No restriction.
17	Northbound	Access only from M11 northbound.
	Southbound	Exit only to M11 southbound.

M1
Belfast – Craigavon

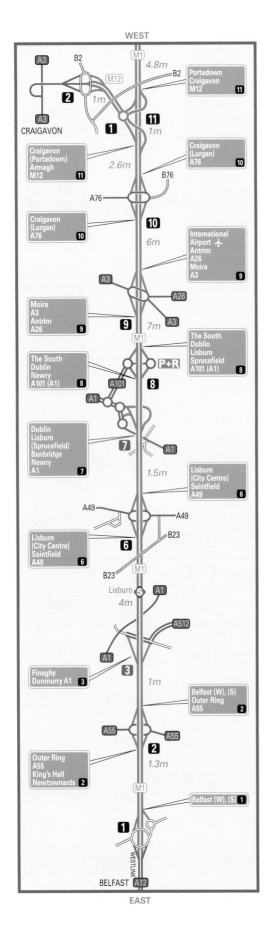

M2, M22
Belfast – Randalstown

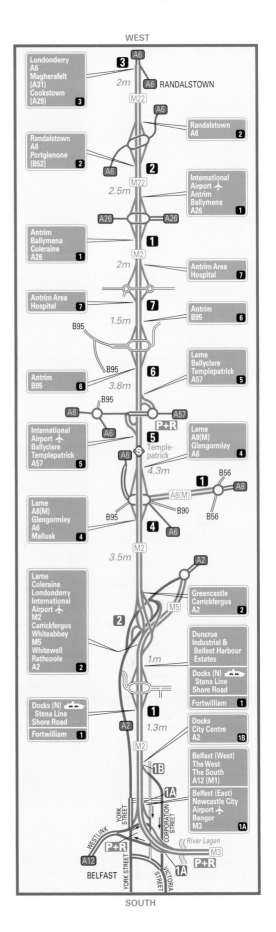

M1
Craigavon – Dungannon

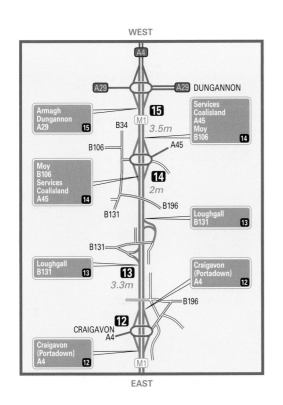

WEST

A4

A29 — A29 DUNGANNON

Armagh
Dungannon
A29 **15**

15

M1

3.5m

B34

B106

A45

Services
Coalisland
A45
Moy
B106 **14**

Moy
B106
Services
Coalisland
A45 **14**

14

2m

B131

B196

Loughgall
B131 **13**

B131

Loughgall
B131 **13**

13

3.3m

Craigavon
(Portadown)
A4 **12**

B196

CRAIGAVON
A4

12

Craigavon
(Portadown)
A4 **12**

M1

EAST

M2
Ballymena Bypass

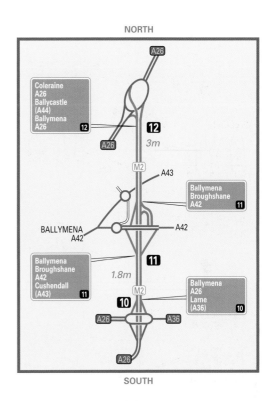

NORTH

A26

Coleraine
A26
Ballycastle
(A44)
Ballymena
A26 **12**

12

A26

3m

M2

A43

Ballymena
Broughshane
A42 **11**

BALLYMENA
A42

A42

Ballymena
Broughshane
A42
Cushendall
(A43) **11**

11

1.8m

M2

Ballymena
A26
Larne
(A36) **10**

10

A26 — A36

10

A26

SOUTH

M50 Dublin Ring Road and Port Tunnel

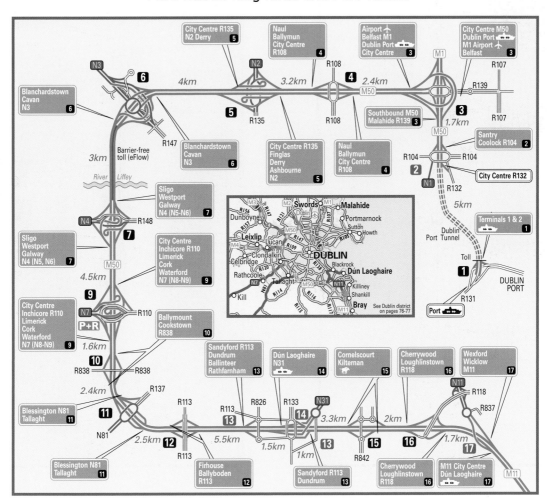

M1
M50 – Drogheda

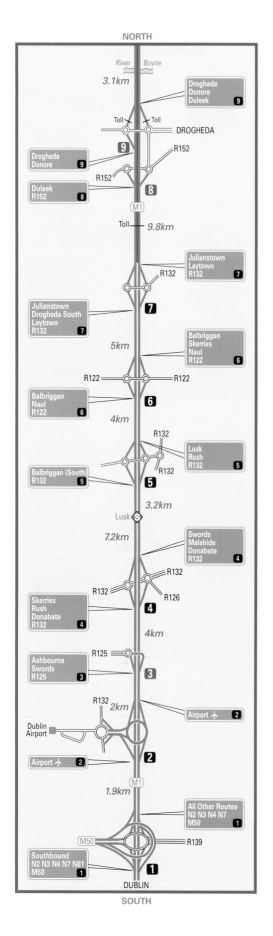

M1
Drogheda – Dundalk

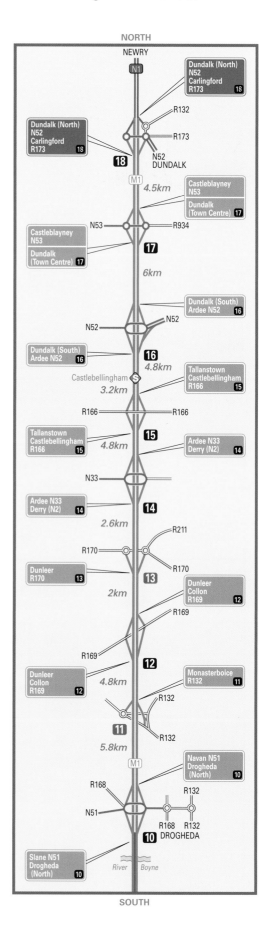

M2
Kilshane Cross – Ashbourne

M3
Clonee – Kells

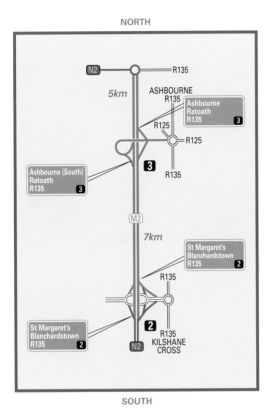

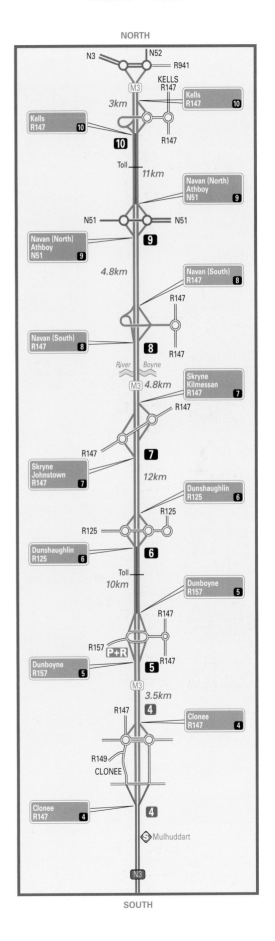

M6
M4 – Athlone

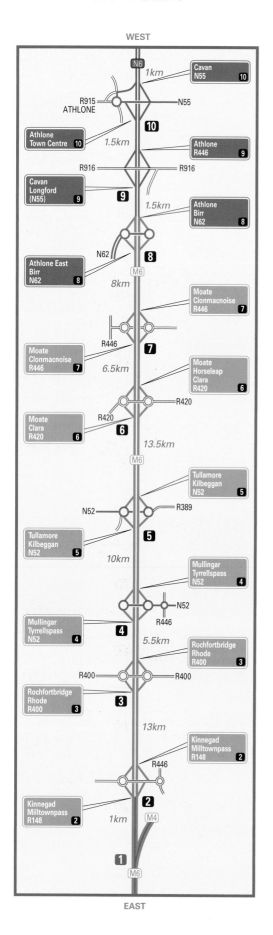

M6
Athlone – Galway

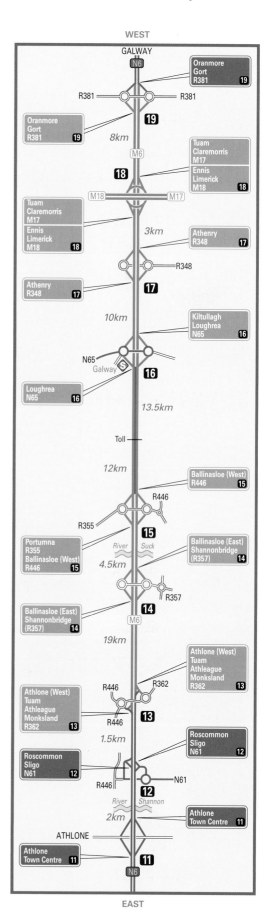

M7
Naas – M8

WEST

Cork
M8   19

11km   19

Toll

R445   4km

Port Laoise
R445   18

Port Laoise
R445   18

18   R445

3.2km

Durrow
Abbeyleix
Port Laoise
N77   17

N77   N77

Durrow
Abbeyleix
Port Laoise
N77   17

17

7km

R445

Port Laoise
Carlow
R445   16

16   R445

Port Laoise
Carlow
R445   16

6km

Mountmellick
Portarlington
Killenard
R422   15

Mountmellick
Portarlington
Killenard
R422   15

15   R445

M7

12.5km   R445

Monasterevin
Athy
Rathangan
R445   14

Junction 14
Mayfield

Monasterevin
Athy
Rathangan
R445   14

14   R445

6.8km

Kildare
Nurney
R415   13

R415   R415

Kildare
Nurney
R415   13

13   R445

6.5km   R413

Newbridge
The Curragh
R445   12

Newbridge
Kilcullen
The Curragh
R445   12

2   R413

M9

12   R445

R448

6km   4.8km

Athy
Kilcullen
Castlecomer
R448   2

11

6km   R445

Waterford
Kilkenny
Carlow
M9   11

Naas
R445   10

R445   10

Newbridge
R445   10

M7   6.5km

NAAS
R445

Naas
R445   9

Naas
R445   9

9

N7

EAST

M7
M8 – Limerick

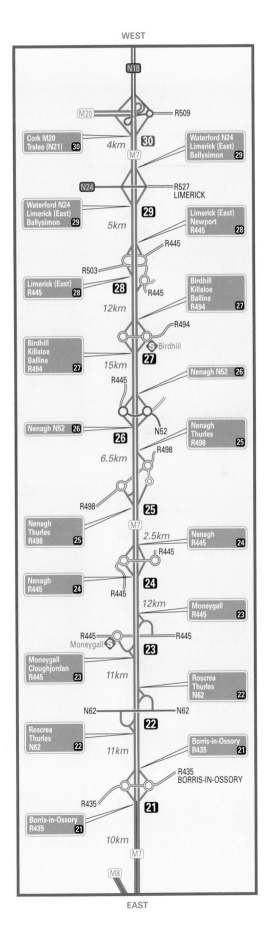

WEST

N18

M20   R509

Cork M20
Tralee (N21)   30

4km   30

Waterford N24
Limerick (East)
Ballysimon   29

M7

N24   R527
LIMERICK

Waterford N24
Limerick (East)
Ballysimon   29

29

Limerick (East)
Newport
R445   28

5km

R445

R503

Limerick (East)
R445   28

28   R445

Birdhill
Killaloe
Ballina
R494   27

12km

R494

Birdhill

Birdhill
Killaloe
Ballina
R494   27

15km   27

Nenagh N52   26

R445

Nenagh N52   26

N52

Nenagh
Thurles
R498   25

26

6.5km   R498

R498

Nenagh
Thurles
R498   25

25

M7

2.5km

Nenagh
R445   24

R445

Nenagh
R445   24

24   R445

12km

Moneygall
R445   23

R445   R445

Moneygall

23

Moneygall
Cloughjordan
R445   23

11km

Roscrea
Thurles
N62   22

N62   N62

22

Roscrea
Thurles
N62   22

Borris-in-Ossory
R435   21

11km

R435
BORRIS-IN-OSSORY

Borris-in-Ossory
R435   21

R435   21

10km

M7

M8

EAST

M8
M7 – Cahir

NORTH

M7

M7

M8

1

6km

Abbeyleix
Rathdowney
Templemore
R433 **3**

R433 ——— R433
Ⓢ Manor Stone

Abbeyleix
Rathdowney
Templemore
R433 **3**

3

17.5km

Kilkenny
Johnstown
Urlingford
R693 **4**

R639
R693
R639

Kilkenny
Johnstown
Urlingford
R693 **4**

4

11km

Thurles N75
Twomileborris **5**

N75 ———

5

7km

Thurles N62
Horse and Jockey
Littleton
Holycross **6**

M8

N62 ——— R639

6

Thurles N62
Horse and Jockey
Littleton
Holycross **6**

11km

Cashel
Dundrum
R639 **7**

R639

R639

7

Cashel
Dundrum
R639 **7**

4km

Cashel
Fethard
Clonmel
R692 **8**

R692

R692
Ⓢ
Cashel

Cashel
Fethard
Clonmel
R692 **8**

R698

8

1.5km

Tipperary N74
Cashel **9**

N74 ———

Tipperary N74
Cashel **9**

9

R639

11km

Limerick N24
Waterford
Cahir **10**

R639

Limerick N24
Waterford
Cahir **10**

10

N24

M8

N24
CAHIR

SOUTH

M8
Cahir – Cork

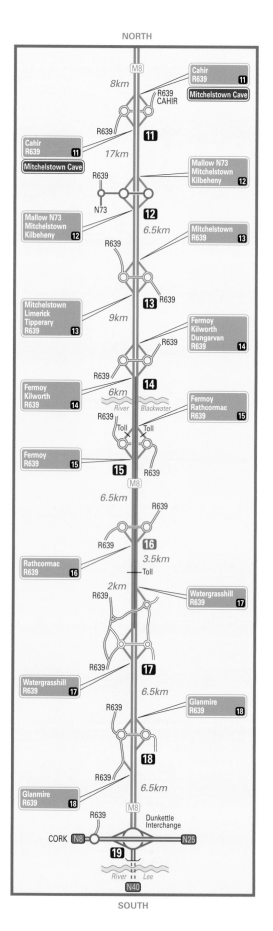

NORTH

M8

8km

Cahir
R639 **11**
Mitchelstown Cave

R639
CAHIR

R639

11

Cahir
R639 **11**
Mitchelstown Cave

17km

Mallow N73
Mitchelstown
Kilbeheny **12**

R639

N73

12

6.5km

Mitchelstown
R639 **13**

Mallow N73
Mitchelstown
Kilbeheny **12**

R639

13 R639

Mitchelstown
Limerick
Tipperary
R639 **13**

9km

Fermoy
Kilworth
Dungarvan
R639 **14**

R639

R639

14

Fermoy
Kilworth
R639 **14**

6km
River   Blackwater

R639

Fermoy
Rathcormac
R639 **15**

Toll   Toll

Fermoy
R639 **15**

15

R639

M8

6.5km

R639

Rathcormac
R639 **16**

R639

16

3.5km

Toll

2km

R639

Watergrasshill
R639 **17**

Watergrasshill
R639 **17**

R639

17

6.5km

Glanmire
R639 **18**

R639

18

Glanmire
R639 **18**

R639

6.5km

M8

R639

Dunkettle
Interchange

CORK N8

N25

19

River   Lee
N40

SOUTH

M11
Dublin – Ashford

NORTH

M50

DUBLIN
N11

R837

1km

City Centre M11
Dún Laoghaire   17

17

M11

2.2km

Bray North
R761   5

R119

5

Bray
Shankill   5

R761

Bray
Fassaroe
R918   6

2.1km

R918

Bray
Fassaroe
R918   6

6

19km

Glen of the Downs

N11

Wicklow S

Coynes Cross
R772   14

R772

R772

14

Coynes Cross
R772   14

M11

2km

R772

Ashford
R772   15

15

R772
ASHFORD

M11

3km

SOUTH

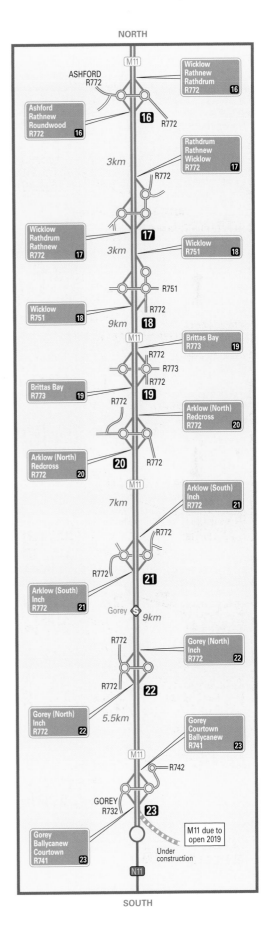

M11
Ashford – Gorey

NORTH

M11

ASHFORD
R772

Wicklow
Rathnew
Rathdrum
R772   16

16

Ashford
Rathnew
Roundwood
R772   16

R772

3km

Rathdrum
Rathnew
Wicklow
R772   17

R772

17

Wicklow
Rathdrum
Rathnew
R772   17

3km

Wicklow
R751   18

R751

Wicklow
R751   18

9km

R772

18

M11

Brittas Bay
R773   19

R772

R773

R772

Brittas Bay
R773   19

19

R772

Arklow (North)
Redcross
R772   20

Arklow (North)
Redcross
R772   20

20

R772

M11

Arklow (South)
Inch
R772   21

7km

R772

R772

21

Arklow (South)
Inch
R772   21

Gorey S   *9km*

R772

Gorey (North)
Inch
R772   22

R772

22

Gorey (North)
Inch
R772   22

5.5km

Gorey
Courtown
Ballycanew
R741   23

M11

R742

GOREY
R732   23

Gorey
Ballycanew
Courtown
R741   23

M11 due to
open 2019

Under
construction

N11

SOUTH

M4
Leixlip – McNead's Bridge

WEST

N4

Coralstown (L1025) **13**

13 Coralstown (L1025) **13**

R148
MCNEAD'S BRIDGE
Royal Canal

8km

M4

Kinnegad Galway R148 (M6) **12**

(M6) R446

12

M6

1.5km

Galway M6 Athlone **11**

11

1.5km

R401
R148
R148

Kinnegad R401 **10**

10 R148

R401

14.3km

Enfield ◆S◆

M4

Edenderry Enfield R402 **9**

3.2km

Toll
R148
R402
Toll
R159

9 R148

Edenderry Enfield R402 **9**

11km

Toll

Clane Killcock Trim R407 **8**

R148

R407

8 R148

Clane Killcock R407

Enfield Maynooth R148 **8**

8km

Naas Maynooth R406 **7**

R406
R406

7

Naas Maynooth R406 **7**

3.8km

Celbridge West Leixlip West R449 **6**

R405
R449
R449
R148

Celbridge West Leixlip West R449 **6**

6

R148

M4

5km
LEIXLIP
R148

R403

Leixlip R148 **5**

Leixlip Celbridge R148 **5**

5

N4

EAST

M9
M7 – Waterford

NORTH

M7

M7

Waterford M9 **1**

M9

1

6km

Kilcullen Kilmead R448 **2**

R418
R448

R448
2

Kilcullen Newbridge R448 **2**

R448

15.5km

Athy Baltinglass N78 **3**

N78
R747

3

Athy Baltinglass N78 **3**

12km

Castledermot Carlow R448 **4**

R448
R448

Castledermot Carlow R448 **4**

4

12km

Carlow Rosslare N80 **5**

Carlow ◆S◆
N80
N80

5

Carlow Rosslare N80 **5**

6.5km

Carlow (South) Bagenalstown Leighlinbridge R448 **6**

R448

Carlow (South) Bagenalstown R448 **6**

6
R448

Paulstown Thomastown Gowran R712 **7**

Paulstown Thomastown Gowran R712 **7**

Paulstown ◆S◆
R912
R712

7

8.8km

Kilkenny N10 **8**

N10

8

Kilkenny N10 **8**

Kilkenny N10 Stoneyford R713 **9**

N10
R713

9.5km

Kilkenny N10 **9**

9

10.2km

Thomastown Knocktopher R699 **10**

R699
R699

10

M9

Thomastown Knocktopher R699 **10**

13.5km

Mullinavat New Ross R704 **11**

R704
R704

11

Mullinavat R704 **11**

11.5km

12
N25 ROSSLARE

LIMERICK CLONMEL N24

R861
WATERFORD

Toll *River Suir*

N25 CORK

SOUTH

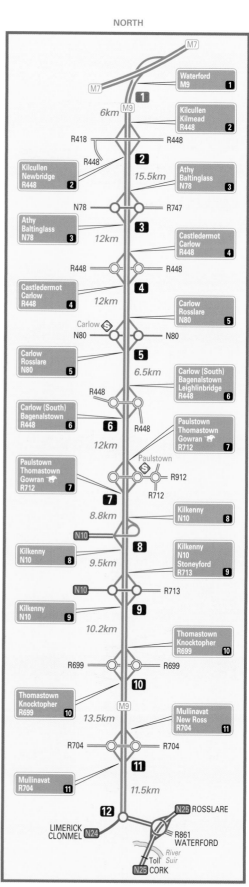

M17, M18
Shannon – Tuam

NORTH

N17 | TUAM R942

N83 — 20

M17

13km

19

Roscommon N63 Baile Chláir R354 — 19

R354 — N63

Roscommon N63 — 19

12km

M17

Dublin Galway M6 — 18

Dublin Galway M6 — 18

M6 | M6

18

M18

Ardrahan Kinvarra Oranmore R458 — 17

14km

R458 — R458

17

Ardrahan Kinvarra Oranmore R458 — 17

13km

Loughrea Gort R380 — 16

R458

Loughrea Gort R380 — 16

R380 — 16

16km

Crusheen R458 — 15

R458

15

R458

6.5km

Crusheen R458 — 15

Ennis (North) Barefield R458 — 14

R458 — 14

Ennis (North) Barefield R458 — 14

3km

Scarriff Tulla R352 — 13

R352 — R352

13

Scarriff Tulla R352 — 13

3km

Ennis N85 Ennistimon Kilrush — 12

N85

12

Ennis N85 Ennistimon Kilrush — 12

R458

Quin Dromoland Ballygirreen R458 — 11

4km

Quin Dromoland Ballygirreen R458 — 11

R458

11

5km

Newmarket on Fergus Carrigoran R472 — 10

R472 — R472

10

Newmarket on Fergus Carrigoran R472 — 10

M18

4km

Shannon N19 ✈ — 9

9

R458

SHANNON N19

Shannon N19 ✈ — 9

N18

SOUTH

M20
Limerick – N21

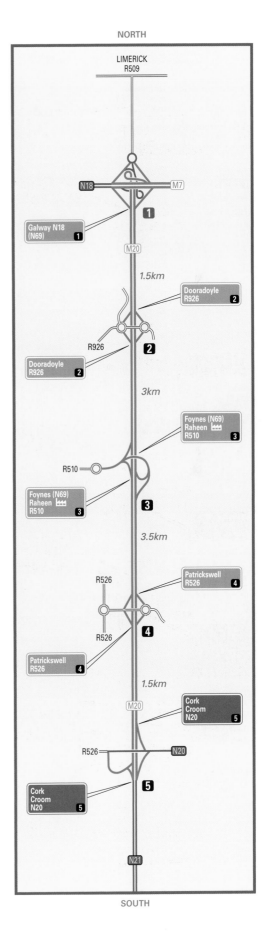

NORTH

LIMERICK R509

N18 | M7

1

Galway N18 (N69) — 1

M20

1.5km

Dooradoyle R926 — 2

R926

2

Dooradoyle R926 — 2

3km

Foynes (N69) Raheen R510 — 3

R510

Foynes (N69) Raheen R510 — 3

3

3.5km

Patrickswell R526 — 4

R526

4

R526

Patrickswell R526 — 4

1.5km

M20

Cork Croom N20 — 5

R526 — N20

Cork Croom N20 — 5

5

N21

SOUTH

Counties and administrative areas

Following recent reform there are 11 local government districts in Northern Ireland. The former six counties of Antrim, Armagh, Down, Fermanagh, Londonderry and Tyrone are still referred to locally but their use is in decline and they have not been used in this atlas.

The Republic of Ireland is divided into 31 administrative districts which includes 26 counties.

All the districts for each country are shown on the following map and listed below, together with the abbreviated name which has been used in the index.

The index lists places appearing in the main-map section of the atlas in alphabetical order. The reference following each name gives the atlas page number and grid reference of the square in which the place appears. More than 75 top places of interest are indexed in **red** or **green** (if a World Heritage site), motorway service areas in **blue**, airports in *blue italic* and National Parks in *green italic*.

Northern Ireland Districts

A & ND	**Ards and North Down**
A & N	**Antrim & Newtownabbey**
AB & C	**Armagh City, Banbridge & Craigavon**
Belfst	**Belfast (1)**
CC & G	**Causeway Coast & Glens**
D & S	**Derry City & Strabane**
E Antr	**Mid & East Antrim**
F & O	**Fermanagh & Omagh**
L & C	**Lisburn & Castlereagh City**
M Ulst	**Mid Ulster**
NM & D	**Newry, Mourne and Down**

Republic of Ireland

C Cork	**Cork City (2)**
C Dubl	**Dublin City (3)**
C Gal	**Galway City (4)**
Carlow	**Carlow**
Cavan	**Cavan**
Clare	**Clare**
Cork	**Cork**
Donegl	**Donegal**
Dublin	**Dublin (Dún Laoghaire-Rathdown/Fingal/South Dublin)**
Galway	**Galway**
Kerry	**Kerry**
Kildre	**Kildare**
Kilken	**Kilkenny**
Laois	**Laois**
Leitrm	**Leitrim**
Limrck	**Limerick (City & County)**
Longfd	**Longford**
Louth	**Louth**
Mayo	**Mayo**
Meath	**Meath**
Monhan	**Monaghan**
Offaly	**Offaly**
Roscom	**Roscommon**
Sligo	**Sligo**
Tippry	**Tipperary**
Watfd	**Waterford (City & County)**
Wmeath	**Westmeath**
Wexfd	**Wexford**
Wicklw	**Wicklow**

A

Abbey Galway......................... 26 H3
Abbeydorney/Mainistir Ó
  d'Torna Kerry................... 16 F10
Abbeyfeale/Mainistir na
  Féile Limrck..................... 17 L9
Abbeyknockmoy Galway..... 34 G5
Abbeylara/Mainistir
  Leathrátha Longfd........... 45 L8
Abbeyleix/Mainistir
  Laoise Laois..................... 29 K7
Abbeyshrule Longfd............ 36 G2
Abington Limrck.................. 19 L4
Acaill/Achill Island Mayo...... 40 D2
Achill Island/Acaill Mayo..... 40 D2
Achill Sound/Gob an
  Choire Mayo..................... 40 F4
Aclare/Áth an Chláir Sligo... 42 F1
Acton AB & C....................... 56 D4
Adamstown Wexfd............... 15 K3
Adare/Áth Dara Limrck........ 18 F5
Adrigole/Eadargóil Cork....... 3 N4
Aghabullogue Cork.............. 11 L9
Aghadowey CC & G............. 67 M8
Aghagallon AB & C............. 62 E10
Aghalee L & C..................... 62 E10
Aghaloora Cavan................. 45 M6
Aghamore Leitrm................ 44 D5
Aghamore Mayo.................. 42 G6
Aghavannagh Wicklw......... 31 K7
Aghnagraigue Laois............ 29 M7
Aglish Tippry...................... 27 M5
Aglish Watfd....................... 13 K6
Aglish/An Eaglais Kerry....... 8 G4
Ahafona Kerry.................... 16 F6
Ahanageely Bridge
  Galway............................. 27 K1
Ahane/ Limrck.................... 19 K3
Ahascragh/Áth Eascrach
  Galway............................. 35 M6
Ahoghill E Antr.................... 62 C2
Aillwee Cave Clare.............. 25 K4
Ailt an Chorráin/
  Burtonport Donegl........... 64 C10
Allen Kildre......................... 38 D9
Allenwood Kildre................. 38 D8
Allihies/Na hAilichí Cork...... 2 H5
Anagaire/Annagary
  Donegl............................. 64 D9
An Baile Mór/Ballymore
  Kerry............................... 8 E5
An Baile Thíos/Ballyhees
  Galway............................. 24 E4
An Bun Beag/Bunbeg
  Donegl............................. 64 E8
An Caiseal/Cashel Mayo...... 40 F3
An Carn Mór/Carnmore
  Galway............................. 34 D8
An Charraig/Carrick
  Donegl............................. 58 C7
An Cheathrú Rua/
  Carraroe Galway.............. 33 J9
An Chlais/Clash Kerry.......... 8 E2
An Chlochbhuaile/
  Cloghbolie Donegl........... 58 H1
An Chorrchloch/Corclogh
  Mayo............................... 48 E4
An Clochán/Cloghan
  Donegl............................. 59 M3
An Clochán/Cloghane
  Kerry............................... 8 G2
An Clochán Liath/
  Dunglow/Dungloe
  Donegl............................. 64 D10
An Daingean/Daingean Uí
  Chúis/Dingle Kerry........... 8 E4
An Dúchoraidh/
  Doocharry Donegl............ 59 J1
An Eachléim/Anghleam
  Mayo............................... 48 D7
An Eaglais/Aglish Kerry....... 8 G4
An Fál Carrach/Falcarragh
  Donegl............................. 64 G6
An Fhairche/Clonbur
  Galway............................. 33 M2
An Fód Dubh/Blacksod
  Mayo............................... 48 D8
Anghleam/An Eachléim
  Mayo............................... 48 D7
Annacarty Tippry................. 19 Q5
Annaclone AB & C............... 56 F4
Annacloy NM & D................ 57 L3
Annacurragh Wicklw........... 31 L9
Annagary/Anagaire
  Donegl............................. 64 D9
Annagassan Louth.............. 47 L5
Annagh Cross Galway......... 34 F5

Annahilt L & C..................... 56 H1
Annalong NM & D................ 57 K9
Annalore/Áth an Lobhair
  Monhan............................ 54 F7
Annascaul/Abhainn an
  Scáil Kerry....................... 8 H4
Annestown Watfd................ 14 B9
Ann Mount Dublin............... 39 K9
Annsborough NM & D......... 57 K5
An Rinn/Ringville Watfd....... 13 N7
An Spidéal/Spiddal Galway.. 33 N9
An tEaden Anfach/
  Edenfinfreagh Donegl...... 59 J4
An Tearmann/Termon
  Donegl............................. 65 L8
An tOilean Mór/Bere or
  Bear Island Cork.............. 3 L6
Antrim A & N...................... 62 E5
An tSraith/Srah Mayo......... 48 F6
Araglin Tippry..................... 12 F3
Árainn Mhór/Arranmore/
  Aran Island Donegl.......... 64 B9
Aran Islands/Oileáin
  Árann Galway................... 24 B3
Ardacluggin Cork................. 3 J5
Ardagh Cork....................... 3 L6
Ardagh Meath.................... 46 F4
Ardagh/Ardach Limrck........ 17 P7
Ardagh/Ardach Longfd....... 44 H10
Ardamadane Cork............... 11 Q9
Ardara/Ard an Rátha
  Donegl............................. 58 F4
Ardattin/Ard Aitinn
  Carlow............................. 22 F1
Ardbear Galway.................. 32 D4
Ardclough Kildre................. 38 H8
Ardcrony Tippry.................. 27 L7
Ardee/Baile Átha Fhirdhia
  Louth............................... 47 J5
Ardfert/Ard Fhearta Kerry... 16 D10
Ardfinnan/Ard Fhíonáin
  Tippry.............................. 13 J1
Ardgehane Cork.................. 5 L7
Ardglass Cork..................... 12 E8
Ardglass NM & D................ 57 P5
Ardgroom/Dhá Dhrom
  Cork................................ 3 K3
Ardmore/Aird Mhór Watfd... 7 N3
Ardnacrusha Clare............... 18 H2
Ardoughan Mayo................ 50 F8
Ardpatrick/Ard Pádraig
  Limrck............................. 19 J10
Ardrahan/Ard Raithin
  Galway............................. 26 C2
Ardress AB & C................... 55 P1
Ardrumkilla Galway............. 34 D3
Ardsillish Bridge Wicklw..... 30 F5
Ards Peninsula A & ND........ 63 Q9
Ardstraw D & S................... 60 D5
Ardtanagh AB & C.............. 56 H1
Arigna Roscom................... 52 H10
Arklow/An tInbhear Mór
  Wicklw............................. 31 N10
Armagh AB & C................... 55 N3
Armaghbrague AB & C........ 55 N6
Armoy CC & G.................... 68 B6
Arney F & O........................ 53 P5
Arranmore/Aran Island/
  Árainn Mhór Donegl......... 64 B9
Arthurstown Wexfd............. 14 G6
Articlave CC & G................. 67 K6
Artigarvan D & S................. 60 E2
Arvagh/Ármhach Cavan...... 45 J4
Ashbourne/Cill Dhéagláin
  Meath.............................. 39 K3
Ashfield AB & C.................. 56 F2
Ashford Limrck.................... 17 P10
Ashford/Áth na
  Fuinseoige Wicklw........... 31 P5
Askamore Wexfd................. 23 J3
Askanagap Wicklw.............. 31 K8
Askeaton/Eas Géitine
  Limrck............................. 18 C4
Athboy/Baile Átha Buí
  Meath.............................. 38 C1
Athea/Áth an tSléibhe
  Limrck............................. 17 L7
Athenry/Baile Átha an Rí
  Galway............................. 34 G8
Athgarvan Kildre................. 30 E2
Athlacca Limrck.................. 18 H8
Athleague/Áth Liag
  Roscom............................ 35 N2
Athlone/Baile Átha Luain
  Wmeath............................ 36 C5
Athy Kildre......................... 30 B6
Attanagh Laois................... 29 K9
Attical NM & D................... 56 H9
Attipierce Galway............... 26 G4

Attymass/Áth Tí an
  Mheasaigh Mayo.............. 42 C1
Attymon Galway................. 34 H8
Aughacasla Kerry................ 9 K2
Aughagower Mayo.............. 41 M7
Augher M Ulst.................... 54 G2
Aughnacliffe/Achadh na
  Cloiche Longfd................. 45 J6
Aughnacloy M Ulst............. 55 J2
Aughnagurgan AB & C........ 55 N7
Aughrim Clare..................... 25 N5
Aughrim/Eachroim Galway.. 35 M8
Aughrim/Eachroim Wicklw.. 31 L9
Aviva Stadium C Dubl.......... 39 M7
Avoca/Abhóca Wicklw......... 31 N9

B

Baconstown Meath.............. 38 D5
Bagenalstown/Muine
  Bheag Carlow................... 22 C2
Baile an Fheirtéaraigh/
  Ballyferriter Kerry............ 8 D4
Baile an Mhuilinn/
  Milltown Kerry................. 8 E4
Baile an Sceilg/
  Ballinskelligs Kerry.......... 2 E1
Baile Árd Galway............... 33 N9
Baile Bhuirne/
  Ballyvourney Cork............ 10 F9
Baile Chláir/Claregalway
  Galway............................. 34 D7
Baile Mhic Íre/
  Ballymakeery Cork........... 10 G9
Baile na Finne/Fintown
  Donegl............................. 59 K2
Baile na nGall/
  Ballynaghall Kerry............ 8 D3
Baile Órthaí/Oristown
  Meath.............................. 46 E8
Bailieborough/Coill an
  Chollaigh Cavan.............. 46 C4
Balbriggan/Baile Brigín
  Dublin.............................. 39 N1
Baldwinstown Wexfd........... 15 M6
Balla Mayo......................... 42 C7
Ballacolla Laois.................. 29 J8
Ballagh Tippry.................... 20 C5
Ballaghaderreen/Bealach
  an Doirín Roscom............ 43 K5
Ballaghboy Clare................ 25 N9
Ballaghderg Donegl............ 65 M9
Ballaghkeen Wexfd............. 23 K7
Ballaghmore Laois.............. 28 F6
Ballapousta Louth.............. 46 H6
Ballina Tippry..................... 26 H10
Ballina/Béal an Átha Mayo.. 50 F8
Ballinaclash Wicklw............ 31 M7
Ballinacourty Limrck........... 19 K2
Ballinacurra Cork............... 5 N2
Ballinafad/Béal an Átha
  Fada Sligo........................ 43 N2
Ballinagall Monhan............. 55 J6
Ballinagar Offaly................. 37 L9
Ballinagh/Béal Átha na
  nEach Cavan.................... 45 L4
Ballinahinch Tippry............. 19 L1
Ballinakill/Baile na Coille
  Laois............................... 29 L8
Ballinalack Wmeath............ 37 K1
Ballinalee/Béal Átha na
  Lao Longfd....................... 44 H7
Ballinamallard F & O........... 53 Q2
Ballinameen Roscom........... 43 P5
Ballinamore/Béal an Átha
  Móir Leitrm...................... 44 F1
Ballinamore Bridge
  Galway............................. 35 M4
Ballinamuck Longfd............ 44 G5
Ballinamult Watfd............... 13 L3
Ballinascarty Cork.............. 5 L5
Ballinasleva Mayo.............. 42 B2
Ballinasloe/Béal Átha na
  Sluaighe Galway.............. 35 P7
Ballinbay Bridge Louth....... 47 J1
Ballinclea Wicklw................ 31 P8
Ballincollig/Baile an
  Chollaigh Cork................. 11 P10
Ballindaggan Wexfd............ 22 F5
Ballinderreen/Baile an
  Doirín Galway.................. 25 N1
Ballindine/Baile an
  Daighin Mayo.................. 42 E10
Ballinea Wmeath................ 37 K3
Ballineen/Béal Átha
  Fhínín Cork..................... 5 J4
Ballingarrane Limrck........... 18 D6
Ballingarry Tippry............... 27 N5

Ballingarry/Baile an
  Gharraí Limrck................. 18 E7
Ballingarry/Baile an
  Gharraí Tippry.................. 21 J5
Ballingeary/Béal Átha an
  Ghaorthaidh Cork............ 4 F1
Ballinhassig Cork............... 6 B6
Ballinlough Galway............. 26 H4
Ballinlough Meath.............. 45 Q9
Ballinlough Roscom............ 43 J8
Ballinphunta Sligo.............. 51 P3
Ballinrobe/Baile an Róba
  Mayo............................... 33 P1
Ballinruan Clare................. 25 P7
Ballinskelligs/Baile an
  Sceilg Kerry..................... 2 E1
Ballinspittle/Béal Átha an
  Spidéil Cork.................... 5 P5
Ballintlea Bridge/
  Droichead Bhaile an
  tSléibhe Watfd................. 13 M8
Ballintober Mayo................ 41 P8
Ballintober Roscom............ 43 M9
Ballintogher/Baile an
  Tóchair Sligo.................... 52 E7
Ballintoy CC & G................ 67 Q4
Ballintra/Baile an tSratha
  Donegl............................. 59 K9
Ballinunty Tippry................ 20 G5
Ballinure Galway................ 35 N8
Ballitore/Béal Átha an
  Tuair Kildre...................... 30 D5
Ballivor/Baile Íomhair
  Meath.............................. 38 B3
Ballon/Ballán Carlow.......... 22 E1
Balloo A & ND..................... 63 M10
Ballsmill NM & D................ 56 B10
Ballyagran Limrck............... 18 F9
Ballyallaght CC & G............ 67 P4
Ballybarnes A & ND............ 63 M7
Ballybay/Béal Átha na
  Beithe Monhan................. 55 K8
Ballyboden Dublin.............. 39 L8
Ballybofey/Bealach Féich
  Donegl............................. 59 P4
Ballybogey CC & G............. 67 N6
Ballyboggan Galway........... 35 L7
Ballyboughal/Baile
  Bachaille Dublin.............. 39 L3
Ballyboy Offaly.................. 28 F2
Ballybrittas Laois............... 29 N3
Ballybrophy Laois............... 28 G8
Ballybunion/Baile an
  Bhuinneánaigh Kerry....... 16 F6
Ballycanew/Baile Uí
  Chonnmhai Wexfd........... 23 L4
Ballycarney Wexfd.............. 22 H5
Ballycarry E Antr................ 63 L4
Ballycastle CC & G............. 68 C4
Ballycastle/Baile an
  Chaisil Mayo................... 50 D4
Ballyclare A & N.................. 62 H4
Ballyclerahan Tippry........... 20 F9
Ballyclogh/Baile Cloch
  Cork................................ 11 M4
Ballycloghan Longfd........... 44 G10
Ballycommon Offaly........... 37 L8
Ballycommon Tippry........... 27 K8
Ballyconneely/Baile
  Conaola Galway............... 32 C5
Ballyconnell/Béal Átha
  Conaill Cavan................... 53 Q9
Ballycotton/Baile Choitín
  Cork................................ 7 J6
Ballycrighan Clare.............. 25 P9
Ballycrossaun Galway......... 27 L2
Ballycroy Mayo.................. 40 H2
Ballycroy National Park
  Mayo............................... 49 K9
Ballycullane Wexfd............. 14 H6
Ballycumber/Béal Átha
  Chomair Offaly................ 36 G7
Ballydehob/Béal an dá
  Chab Cork....................... 4 B7
Ballydesmond/Baile
  Deasumna Cork............... 10 F4
Ballydonegan Cork............. 2 H6
Ballyduff Wexfd.................. 23 J4
Ballyduff/An Baile Dubh
  Kerry............................... 16 F7
Ballyduff/An Baile Dubh
  Watfd.............................. 12 G5
Ballyeaston A & N............... 62 H4
Ballyedmond Wexfd............ 23 L6
Ballyfad Wexfd.................... 23 M1
Ballyfarnon/Béal Átha
  Fearnáin Roscom............. 52 G10
Ballyferriter/Baile an
  Fheirtéaraigh Kerry.......... 8 D4

Ballyfin Laois......................... 29 J4
Ballyforan/*Béal Átha*
  Feorainne Roscom 35 N4
Ballyfoyle/*Baile Phóill*
  Kilken 21 N2
Ballygally E Antr.................. 63 K1
Ballygar/*Béal Átha*
  Ghártha Galway 35 M3
Ballygarrett/*Baile*
  Ghearóid Wexfd 23 M5
Ballygarvan Cork 6 C6
Ballygawley M Ulst 54 H1
Ballygawley/*Baile Uí*
  Dhálaigh Sligo 52 D7
Ballygibbon Cork 7 J3
Ballyglass Mayo.................. 42 B8
Ballyglass Mayo.................. 43 J5
Ballygobban Bridge
  Wicklw.............................. 31 K7
Ballygowan A & ND 63 L10
Ballygowan Lower Galway .. 26 H4
Ballyguyroe Cork 11 R2
Ballyhack Wexfd 14 G6
Ballyhahill Limrck 17 M5
Ballyhaise/*Béal Átha hÉis*
  Cavan................................ 45 M1
Ballyhalbert A & ND........... 63 Q10
Ballyhale/*Baile Héil* Kilken ... 21 N7
Ballyhaunis/*Béal Átha*
  hAmhnais Mayo 42 G8
Ballyhea Cork 11 N1
Ballyhean Mayo.................. 41 P7
Ballyheelan Cavan.............. 45 M6
Ballyhees/*An Baile Thíos*
  Galway 24 E4
Ballyheige/*Baile Uí*
  Thaidhg Kerry 16 D9
Ballyhooly/*An Baile Átha*
  hÚlla Cork 12 B5
Ballyhornan NM & D 57 P4
Ballyjamesduff/*Baile*
  Shéamais Dhuibh Cavan .. 45 P5
Ballykelly CC & G 66 G8
Ballykelly Clare 26 D10
Ballyknockan Wicklw......... 31 J3
Ballykockan Beg Wicklw.... 31 P5
Ballylanders Cork............... 6 H6
Ballylanders/*Baile an*
  Londraigh Limrck 19 M10
Ballylaneen Watfd 13 R4
Ballyleague Roscom 44 D10
Ballylevin Donegl 65 P9
Ballylickey Cork 4 C4
Ballyliffin/*Baile Lifín*
  Donegl.............................. 66 B3
Ballylongford/*Béal Átha*
  Longfoirt Kerry 17 J6
Ballylooby Tippry 12 H1
Ballylumford E Antr............ 63 L2
Ballylynan/*Baile Uí*
  Laigheanáin Laois 29 P7
Ballymacarbry Watfd 13 L2
Ballymacoda Cork 7 K4
Ballymaddock Cross Laois .. 29 N5
Ballymadun Dublin 39 K3
Ballymaghroe Wicklw........ 31 P5
Ballymagorry D & S 60 E2
Ballymahon/*Baile Uí*
  Mhatháin Longfd 36 F2
Ballymakeery/*Baile Mhic*
  Íre Cork 10 G9
Ballymanus Bridge Wicklw .. 31 K8
Ballymartin NM & D 57 J9
Ballymartle Cork 6 B7
Ballymascanlan/*Baile*
  Mhic Scanláin Louth........ 47 L1
Ballymena E Antr 62 E2
Ballymoe/*Béal Átha Mó*
  Galway 43 L9
Ballymoney CC & G 67 N7
Ballymoney Wexfd 23 N2
Ballymore Cork 6 F5
Ballymore Donegl 65 K6
Ballymore/*An Baile Mór*
  Kerry 8 E5
Ballymore/*An Baile Mór*
  Wmeath............................ 36 G4
Ballymore Eustace/*An*
  Baile Mór Kildre.............. 30 G2
Ballymote/*Baile an*
  Mhóta Sligo 52 C9
Ballymurn Wexfd 23 J8
Ballymurphy/*Baile Uí*
  Mhurchú Carlow 22 D5
Ballynabola Wexfd............. 14 H4
Ballynabrennagh Lower
  Kerry 9 P1

Ballynacarrow/*Baile na*
  Cora Sligo 51 P7
Ballynacorra Cork 6 G4
Ballynacourty Watfd 13 N6
Ballynaghall/*Baile na*
  nGall Kerry 8 D3
Ballynahinch Kerry 9 P2
Ballynahinch NM & D......... 57 K2
Ballynahown Wmeath....... 36 E7
Ballynakilla Cork 3 L6
Ballyneety Limrck 19 J5
Ballynoe/*An Baile Nua*
  Cork.................................. 12 F7
Ballynure A & N 63 J4
Ballyogan/*Baile Uí Ógain*
  Dublin 39 N9
Ballyorgan Limrck 12 A1
Ballyouskill/*Baile Ascaille*
  Kilken 29 L9
Ballypatrick Tippry 21 J9
Ballyporeen/*Béal Átha*
  Póirín Tippry 12 F2
Ballyragget/*Béal Átha*
  Ragad Kilken 29 L10
Ballyrashane CC & G.......... 67 M6
Ballyroan/*Baile Átha an*
  Róine Laois 29 L7
Ballyrobert A & N 62 H5
Ballyroe Bridge Kildre 30 C7
Ballyronan M Ulst 62 A5
Ballysadore/*Baile Easa*
  Dara Sligo 52 C7
Ballysaggart Watfd 12 H4
Ballyshannon/*Baile*
  Sonnáin Kildre 30 D4
Ballyshannon/*Béal Átha*
  Seanaidh Donegl 59 J10
Ballystrudder E Antr.......... 63 M4
Ballyvary/*Béal Átha*
  Bhearaigh Mayo 42 B5
Ballyvaughan/*Baile Uí*
  Bheacháin Clare 25 K3
Ballyvourney/*Baile*
  Bhuirne Cork 10 F9
Ballyvoy CC & G 68 Q4
Ballywalter A & ND 63 Q9
Ballyweelin Sligo 52 C5
Ballywilliam Wexfd 22 D8
Balnamore CC & G............. 67 N7
Balrothery Dublin 39 M1
Baltimore/*Dún na Séad*
  Cork.................................. 4 C9
Baltinglass/*Bealach*
  Conglais Wicklw............. 30 F7
Baltray/*Baile Trá* Louth 47 M8
Banagher/*Beannchar*
  Offaly 27 P1
Banbridge AB & C.............. 56 E3
Bandon/*Droichead na*
  Bandan Cork 5 M3
Bangor A & ND................... 63 N6
Bangor Abbey A & ND........ 63 N6
Bangor Erris/*Baingear*
  Mayo 49 J7
Bankfield Galway 27 N1
Banoge Limrck 18 G7
Bansha/*An Bháinseach*
  Tippry 20 B8
Banteer/*Bántir* Cork......... 11 K5
Bantry/*Beanntraí* Cork 4 B5
Bantry House & Garden
  Cork.................................. 4 B5
Barefield Clare 25 N8
Barna Limrck 19 M6
Barna/*Bearna* Galway 33 Q9
Barnahown Tippry 12 F3
Barnatra/*Barr na Trá* Mayo .. 48 G5
Barndarrig Wicklw............. 31 P7
Barntown/*Baile an*
  Bharúnaigh Wexfd 15 M4
Barraduff Kerry 10 D6
Barr na Trá/*Barnatra*
  Mayo 48 G5
Barry Longfd 36 F1
Bartlemy Cork 12 D7
Batterjohn Meath 38 F3
Batterstown Meath............ 38 H4
Bá Uachtair/*Boyoughter*
  Donegl.............................. 58 H2
Bawnard Cork 3 K4
Bawnboy Cavan................. 53 P9
Bealagrellagh Kerry........... 9 P2
Béal an Mhuirthead/
  Belmullet Mayo 48 F5
Béal Átha an
  Ghaorthaidh/
  Ballingeary Cork 4 F1
Bealin Wmeath.................. 36 E5
Beara Peninsula Cork 2 H6

Bearna/*Barna* Galway 33 Q9
Beaufort Kerry 9 P6
Bective Abbey Meath 38 F1
Bekan Mayo 42 F8
Belcarra Mayo................... 41 Q7
Belclare Galway 34 D4
Belcoo F & O 53 L5
Belfast Belfst 63 J8
Belfast International
  Airport A & N 62 F6
Belfast Zoo Belfst.............. 63 J6
Belgooly Cork 6 C8
Bellacorick Mayo............... 49 L8
Bellaghy M Ulst 62 B3
Bellanagare/*Béal Átha na*
  gCarr Roscom 43 M6
Bellanaleck F & O 53 P5
Bellanode Monhan 54 H5
Belleek F & O..................... 52 H1
Belleek NM & D 56 B7
Belleek Pottery F & O......... 52 H1
Belleview Louth 47 M8
Bellewstown Meath 47 L10
Belmayne C Dubl............... 39 N5
Belmullet/*Béal an*
  Mhuirthead Mayo 48 F5
Belturbet/*Béal Tairbirt*
  Cavan................................ 54 C9
Belvedere House Wmeath ... 37 L4
Belview Port Kilken 14 F6
Benburb M Ulst.................. 55 M2
Bennettsbridge/
  Droichead Binéid Kilken .. 21 P5
Beragh F & O..................... 60 H9
Bere or Bear Island/*An*
  tOilean Mór Cork 3 L6
Bessbrook NM & D 56 C7
Bettystown/*Baile an*
  Bhiataigh Meath 47 N9
Bilboa Carlow 29 P10
Birdhill Tippry 19 L1
Birdhill Services Tippry 19 L1
Birr/*Biorra* Offaly 28 C3
Birr Castle Gardens &
  Science Centre Offaly 28 C3
Blackditch/*An Clai Dubh*
  Wicklw.............................. 31 P4
Blacklion/*An Blaic* Cavan .. 53 L5
Blackrock C Cork 6 D4
Blackrock Louth 47 L3
Blackrock/*An Charraig*
  Dhubh Dublin 39 N8
Blacksod/*An Fód Dubh*
  Mayo 48 D8
Blackwater/*An Abhainn*
  Dubh Wexfd 23 L8
Blackwatertown AB & C..... 55 M2
Blanchardstown Dublin...... 39 K6
Blarney/*An Bhlarna* Cork ... 11 Q9
Blarney Castle Cork 11 Q9
Bleary AB & C 56 D2
Blennerville/*Cathair Uí*
  Mhóráin Kerry 9 N2
Blessington/*Baile Coimín*
  Wicklw.............................. 30 H2
Blue Ball Offaly................. 36 H10
Bockagh Roscom 43 K4
Bodyke Clare..................... 26 E8
Bofeenaun Mayo............... 41 P3
Boherboy/*Bóthar Buí*
  Kerry 8 D3
Boherbue Cork 10 H4
Bohernabreena Dublin....... 39 K8
Boho F & O 53 M4
Bohola/*Both Chomhla*
  Mayo 42 D4
Boleynass Wicklw............. 31 N5
Boolavogue/*Baile*
  Mhaodhóg Wexfd............ 23 K5
Boolybane Cork 4 E8
Borcarnagh Cork 3 Q4
Borris/*An Bhuiríos* Carlow .. 22 C4
Borris-in-Ossory/*Buiríos*
  Mór Osraí Laois 28 F7
Borrisokane/*Buiríos Uí*
  Chéin Tippry 27 M6
Borrisoleigh Tippry 20 C1
Bóthar Buí/*Boherboy*
  Kerry 8 D3
Boyle/*Mainistir na Búille*
  Roscom 43 P3
Boyne Valley/*Brú na*
  Bóinne Meath 47 K9
Boyoughter/*Bá Uachtair*
  Donegl.............................. 58 H2
Boytown Mayo 50 D3
Brandon Mountain/*Cnoc*
  Bréanainn Kerry 8 F2
Bray/*Bré* Wicklw.............. 39 P10

Bready D & S...................... 60 E1
Breaghwy/*Bréachmhaigh*
  Mayo 41 Q6
Bree/*Brí* Wexfd 22 G8
Bridebridge Cork 12 D6
Bridge End Donegl............. 58 G6
Bridgend Donegl................ 66 B8
Bridgetown Clare 19 J1
Bridgetown Donegl 59 K8
Bridgetown Donegl 65 Q9
Bridgetown/*Baile an*
  Droichid Wexfd 15 M7
Brinlack/*Bun na Leaca*
  Donegl.............................. 64 E6
Brittas Dublin 39 J9
Broadford Kildre 38 B5
Broadford/*Áth Leathen*
  Clare 26 E10
Broadford/*Béal an Átha*
  Limrck 18 C10
Broadway Wexfd 15 Q7
Brookeborough F & O......... 54 C4
Brooklodge Cork 6 D3
Brookville Tippry 19 P8
Brosna Kerry 10 E1
Brosna Offaly 28 C6
Broughshane E Antr........... 62 F1
Bruckless/*An Bhroclais*
  Donegl.............................. 58 F7
Bruff/*An Brú* Limrck......... 19 J7
Brú na Bóinne/Boyne
  Valley Meath 47 K9
Bruree/*Brú Rí* Limrck 18 G8
Brusna Roscom 43 J4
Bryansford NM & D 57 J6
Buckna E Antr 62 G1
Bullaun Galway 35 J9
Buloughera Clare 17 M2
Bunacurry/*Bun an*
  Churraigh Mayo 40 E3
Bun an Churraigh/
  Bunacurry Mayo 40 E3
Bunbeg/*An Bun Beag*
  Donegl.............................. 64 E8
Bunbrosna Wmeath........... 37 K1
Bunclody/*Bun Clóidi*
  Wexfd 22 G3
Buncrana/*Bun Cranncha*
  Donegl.............................. 65 Q6
Bundoran/*Bun Dobhráin*
  Donegl.............................. 52 F1
Bunmahon/*Bun Machan*
  Watfd 14 A9
Bun na hAbhna/
  Bunnahowen Mayo.......... 48 G6
Bunnahowen/*Bun na*
  hAbhna Mayo 48 G6
Bun na Leaca/*Brinlack*
  Donegl.............................. 64 E6
Bunnanaddan/*Bun an*
  Fhendáin Sligo 43 K1
Bunnyconnellan Mayo....... 50 H8
Bunratty Clare................... 18 E2
Bunratty Castle & Folk
  Park Clare 18 F2
Burke Court Galway 27 K5
Burke's Cross Laois 28 H5
Burncourt Tippry 12 F1
Burnfoot CC & G................ 66 H10
Burnfoot/*Bun na*
  hAbhann Donegl............. 66 B8
Burnside A & N 62 H4
Burren Mayo 41 P4
Burren National Park Clare .. 25 M5
Burren Perfumery Clare 25 L5
Burtonport/*Ailt an*
  Chorráin Donegl............. 64 C10
Bushmills CC & G.............. 67 N4
Butlers Bridge/*Droichead*
  an Bhuitléaraigh Cavan .. 45 M1
Butlerstown Cork 5 M7
Buttevant/*Cill na Mallach*
  Cork.................................. 11 N3
Bweeng/*Na Boinn* Cork 11 M7

C

Cadamstown Offaly............ 28 F3
Caherconlish/*Cathair*
  Chinn Lis Limrck 19 K5
Caherdaniel/*Cathair*
  Dónall Kerry 2 G3
Cahergarriff Cork 3 J6
Caherlistrane Galway 34 C4
Cahersiveen/*Cathair*
  Saidhbhín Kerry 8 F9
Cahir/*Án Chathair* Tippry ... 20 D10
Cahore/*Cathóir* Wexfd 23 N5

Caim Wexfd 22 F6
Caladh Thaidhg Galway 33 J9
Caledon M Ulst 55 L3
Callan/Callain Kilken 21 L6
Caltra Galway 35 L5
Calverstown/Baile an
  Chalbhaigh Kildre 30 E4
Camaross/Camross Wexfd 15 K4
Camlough NM & D 56 C7
Camolin/Cam Eolaing
  Wexfd 23 K4
Camp Kerry 9 K3
Campile/Ceann Poill
  Wexfd 14 G5
Canningstown Cavan 46 B3
Cape Clear Island/Oileán
  Chléire Cork 4 B10
Cappagh Cork 5 Q4
Cappagh Beg Clare 25 N8
Cappagh Bridge Galway 27 J3
Cappagh More Clare 25 N8
Cappaghmore Roscom 36 C6
Cappagowlaun Galway 32 F1
Cappaleigh South Cork 3 N5
Cappalusk Galway 35 J6
Cappamore/An Cheapach
  Mhór Limrck 19 M4
Cappavilla Clare 19 J3
Cappawhite/An
  Cheapach Tippry 19 P5
Cappoquin/Ceapach
  Choinn Watfd 13 K5
Carbury Kildre 38 B7
Cardy A & ND 63 P8
Cargahdoo Monhan 55 M10
Cargan E Antr 68 D9
Carland M Ulst 61 N9
Carlanstown Meath 46 E8
Carlingford/Cairlinn Louth .. 47 N1
Carlow/Ceatharlach
  Carlow 30 C9
Carlow Services Carlow ... 30 D10
Carna Galway 32 F7
Carnacon Mayo 41 Q8
Carnalbanagh E Antr 62 H1
Carnaross Meath 46 C8
Carncastle E Antr 63 K1
Carndonagh/Carn
  Domhnach Donegl 66 D4
Carnew/Carn an Bhua
  Wicklw 23 J2
Carney/Fearann Uí
  Chearnaigh Sligo 52 C4
Carnlough E Antr 68 F9
Carnmore/An Carn Mór
  Galway 34 D8
Carnteel M Ulst 55 J2
Carrabane/An Ceathrú
  Bán Galway 34 H10
Carracastle Mayo 42 H3
Carragh Kildre 38 E9
Carraholly Mayo 41 L6
Carraig Airt/Carrigart
  Donegl 65 L5
Carran Clare 25 L5
Carraroe/An Cheathrú
  Rua Galway 33 J9
Carrauntoohil Kerry 9 N8
Carrick/An Charraig
  Donegl 58 C7
Carrick/An Charraig
  Wexfd 15 K6
Carrick-a-Rede Rope
  Bridge CC & G 68 B4
Carrickboy Longfd 36 G1
Carrickfergus E Antr 63 L5
Carrickfergus Castle
  E Antr 63 L5
Carrickmacross/Carraig
  Mhachaire Rois Monhan 46 F3
Carrickmore F & O 61 K8
Carrick-on-Shannon/Cora
  Droma Rúisc Leitrm 44 B4
Carrick-on-Suir/Carraig
  na Siúire Tippry 21 K10
Carrigaholt Clare 16 E4
Carrigaline/Carraig Uí
  Leighin Cork 6 D6
Carrigallen/Carraig Álainn
  Leitrm 44 H3
Carriganimmy Cork 10 H8
Carriganore Watfd 14 D6
Carrigans/An Carraigín
  Donegl 66 B10
Carrigart/Carraig Airt
  Donegl 65 L5
Carrigkerry Limrck 17 N7
Carrigmore Cork 5 J4
Carrignavar Cork 6 C2

Carrigtwohill/Carraig
  Thuathail Cork 6 F4
Carrowdore A & ND 63 P8
Carrowkennedy/Ceathrú
  Chinnéide Mayo 41 L9
Carrowteige/Ceathrú
  Thaidhg Mayo 48 H3
Carrybridge F & O 53 Q5
Carryduff L & C 63 K9
Cartron More Roscom 43 K5
Casey Donegl 65 J5
Cashel/An Caiseal Mayo 40 F3
Cashel/An Caiseal Tippry ... 20 D6
Cashel Cross Laois 29 L6
Cashellahenny Mayo 43 J5
Cashel Services Tippry 20 D7
Casla/Costelloe Galway 33 K8
Castlebaldwin/Béal Átha
  na gCarraigíní Sligo 52 E10
Castlebar/Caisleán an
  Bharraigh Mayo 41 P5
Castlebellingham/Baile
  an Ghearlánaigh Louth 47 L4
Castlebellingham
  Services Louth 47 K4
Castleblakeney/Gallach
  Galway 35 K5
Castleblayney/Baile na
  Lorgan Monhan 55 M9
Castlebridge/Droichead
  an Chaisleáin Wexfd 15 P3
Castlecaulfield M Ulst 61 N10
Castlecomer/Caisleán an
  Chomair Kilken 29 M10
Castleconnell/Caisleán Uí
  Chonaill Limrck 19 K2
Castle Coole F & O 53 Q4
Castlecoote Roscom 35 N1
Castlecor Cork 11 M3
Castlecor Meath 45 P7
Castlecove Kerry 2 H2
Castlecuff Cross Laois 28 G2
Castledaly Wmeath 36 E6
Castledawson M Ulst 62 A4
Castlederg D & S 60 C6
Castledermot/Díseart
  Diarmada Kildre 30 D7
Castledockrell Wexfd 22 G5
Castlefinn/Caisleán na
  Finne Donegl 60 C3
Castlegregory/Caisleán
  Ghriaire Kerry 9 J2
Castleisland/Oileán
  Ciarraí Kerry 10 C3
Castleknock Dublin 39 K6
Castle Lambert Galway 34 F8
Castlelyons/Caisleán Ó
  Liatháin Cork 12 D6
Castlemagner Cork 11 L4
Castlemaine/Caisleán na
  Mainge Kerry 9 N4
Castlemartyr/Baile na
  Martra Cork 7 J4
Castleplunket Roscom 43 N8
Castlepollard/Baile na
  gCros Wmeath 45 N9
Castlerea/An Caisleán
  Riabhach Roscom 43 L8
Castlerock CC & G 67 K5
Castletown Clare 25 L5
Castletown Cork 5 J3
Castletown Cork 6 C8
Castletown Limrck 18 E8
Castletown Wexfd 23 N1
Castletown Wmeath 45 M8
Castletown/Baile an
  Chaisleáin Laois 28 H6
Castletownbere/
  Castletown Berehaven/
  Baile Chaisleán Bhearra
  Cork 3 K5
Castletown Berehaven/
  Castletownbere/
  Baile Chaisleán Bhearra Cork . 3 K5
Castletown Geoghegan/
  Baile Chaisleáin na
  nGeochagán Wmeath 37 J5
Castletown House Kildre .. 38 H7
Castletownroche/Baile
  Chaisleáin an Róistigh
  Cork 12 A4
Castletownshend/Baile
  an Chaisleáin Cork 4 F8
Castle Ward NM & D 57 P3
Castlewarren Kilken 21 Q2
Castlewellan NM & D 57 J5
Castlewellan Forest Park
  NM & D 57 J5
Castlewood Cross Laois ... 29 K9

Cathair Dónall/
  Caherdaniel Kerry 2 G3
Causeway/An Tóchar
  Kerry 16 E8
Cavan/An Cabhán Cavan ... 45 M3
Ceann Trá/Ventry Kerry 8 D4
Ceathrú Thaidhg/
  Carrowteige Mayo 48 H3
Céide Fields Mayo 49 M3
Celbridge/Cill Droichid
  Kildre 38 H7
Chapeltown Kerry 8 D9
Chapeltown NM & D 57 P4
Charlemont AB & C 55 N1
Charlestown/Baile
  Chathail Mayo 42 G3
Charleville/Ráth Luirc
  Cork 18 G10
Chester Beatty Library
  C Dubl 39 M7
Christ Church Cathedral
  C Dubl 39 M7
Church Bay CC & G 68 C2
Churchtown Cork 6 H4
Churchtown Cork 6 H6
Churchtown Donegl 60 D3
Churchtown Limrck 17 P8
Churchtown Wexfd 14 G9
Churchtown Wexfd 15 Q7
Churchtown/Baile an
  Teampaill Cork 11 N2
Cill Charthaigh/Kilcar
  Donegl 58 D7
Cill Chiaráin/Kilkieran
  Galway 32 G7
Cill Rónáin/Kilronan
  Galway 24 C3
Cill Ulta/Killult Donegl 64 G6
Cionn Caslach/
  Kincaslough Donegl 64 C9
City of Derry Airport D & S .. 66 E8
Clabby F & O 54 D2
Claddaghduff Galway 32 B2
Clady A & N 62 F6
Clady D & S 60 C4
Clady M Ulst 62 B2
Clahane Kerry 9 N2
Clane/Claonadh Kildre 38 F8
Clara/Clóirtheach Offaly ... 36 H7
Claran Galway 33 Q4
Clarecastle/Droichead an
  Chláir Clare 25 M10
Claregalway/Baile Chláir
  Galway 34 D7
Clare Island Mayo 40 E6
Claremorris/Clár Chlainne
  Mhuiris Mayo 42 D9
Clarina Limrck 18 G4
Clarinbridge/Droichead
  an Chláirín Galway 34 E9
Clash/An Chlais Kerry 8 E2
Clash Cross Laois 29 J7
Clashmore/Clais Mhór
  Watfd 13 K8
Classes Lake Cork 11 P10
Claudy D & S 60 H1
Cleggan/An Cloigeann
  Galway 32 C2
Cleristown Wexfd 15 M6
Clifden/An Clochán Galway . 32 D3
Cliffoney/Cliafuine Sligo ... 52 D2
Cliffs of Moher Clare 24 F6
Clogagh Cork 5 L5
Clogh E Antr 68 B10
Clogh Laois 28 H8
Clogh/An Chloch Kilken 29 N9
Cloghan Wmeath 37 N2
Cloghan/An Clochán
  Donegl 59 M3
Cloghan/An Clochán
  Offaly 36 D10
Cloghane/An Clochán
  Kerry 8 G2
Cloghbolie/An
  Chlochbhuaile Donegl 58 H1
Clogheen/An Cloichín
  Tippry 12 H2
Clogher M Ulst 54 F2
Clogher Mayo 41 M6
Clogher Mayo 41 Q8
Clogher Roscom 44 B9
Clogherane Kerry 3 M3
Clogherhead/Ceann
  Chlochair Louth 47 N7
Clogh Mills CC & G 68 B9
Cloghroe Cork 11 P10
Clohamon/Cloch Ámainn
  Wexfd 22 G4

Clologe/Cloch Cúirte
  Wexfd 23 K4
Clonaghadoo Laois 29 K2
Clonakenny Tippry 28 D8
Clonakilty/Cloich na
  Coillte Cork 5 K6
Clonalis House Roscom 43 L7
Clonard Meath 37 Q4
Clonaslee/Cluain na Slí
  Laois 28 H2
Clonbulloge/Cluain Bolg
  Offaly 37 Q9
Clonbur/An Fhairche
  Galway 33 M2
Clondalkin Dublin 39 K7
Clondrohid/Cluain
  Droichead Cork 10 H9
Clondulane Cork 12 D5
Clonea Watfd 13 Q2
Clonee Meath 39 J5
Cloneen Tippry 20 H7
Clonegall/Cluain na nGall
  Carlow 22 G2
Clonenagh Cross Laois 29 J5
Clones/Cluain Eois
  Monhan 54 F7
Clongeen Wexfd 15 J5
Clonglaskan Cork 3 J6
Clonigulane Clare 17 L1
Clonlara/Cluain Lára Clare . 19 J2
Clonmacnoise/Cluain
  Mnic Nóis Offaly 36 C7
Clonmacnoise Monastery
  Offaly 36 C7
Clonmany/Cluain Maine
  Donegl 66 B3
Clonmel/Cluain Meala
  Tippry 20 G10
Clonmellon/Ráistín
  Wmeath 46 C10
Clonmore Carlow 30 H9
Clonmore Louth 47 M6
Clonoghil Cross Laois 28 G6
Clonoulty Tippry 20 C4
Clonroche/Cluain an
  Róistigh Wexfd 22 F8
Clonsilla Dublin 39 K6
Clontarf C Dubl 39 N6
Clontibret Monhan 55 L7
Clontubrid Kilken 21 L1
Clonvaraghan NM & D 57 J4
Clonygowan/Cluain na
  nGamhan Offaly 29 L1
Cloonagh Galway 32 E1
Cloonbeggaun Roscom ... 36 B7
Cloondara/Cluain Dá
  Ráth Longfd 44 E8
Clooney Clare 25 P9
Cloonfad/Cluain Fada
  Roscom 42 H9
Cloonfada Clare 26 G10
Clooniff Roscom 36 B7
Cloonkeen Kerry 10 E8
Cloonkeevy/Cluain
  Ciabhaigh Sligo 51 P9
Cloonnagro Clare 26 D6
Cloontuskert Roscom 44 C9
Clough NM & D 57 L4
Clough/An Chloch Wexfd .. 23 L3
Cloughjordan/Cloch
  Shiurdáin Tippry 27 N7
Cloyne/Cluain Cork 6 H5
Clydagh Cork 3 M5
Cnocán na Líne/
  Knocknalina Mayo 48 G4
Cnoc Bréanainn/Brandon
  Mountain Kerry 8 F2
Coachford/Áth an
  Chóiste Cork 11 M10
Coagh M Ulst 61 Q7
Coalisland M Ulst 61 P9
Cobh/An Cóbh Cork 6 E2
Colehill Longfd 36 G1
Coleraine CC & G 67 L6
Colliga Wicklw 30 H6
Collinstown/Baile na
  gCailleach Wmeath 45 P10
Collon/Collann Louth 47 J7
Collooney/Cúil Mhuine
  Sligo 52 C7
Comber A & ND 63 M9
Common Bridge Donegl ... 58 F5
Conahy Kilken 21 M1
Cong/Conga Mayo 33 N2
Conlig A & ND 63 M7
Conna Cork 12 F6
Connemara National Park
  Galway 32 E2
Connor E Antr 62 F3

Convoy/*Conmhaigh* Donegl ... 60 B2
Coogue Mayo ... 42 F7
Cookstown M Ulst ... 61 P7
Coolaney/*Cúil Áine* Sligo ... 51 P6
Coolboy Donegl ... 65 M9
Coolboy Wicklw ... 23 J1
Coolcap Cork ... 7 J3
Coolcoosaun Clare ... 26 F7
Coolderry Offaly ... 28 D5
Coole Tippry ... 26 H8
Coole/*An Chúil* Wmeath ... 45 M9
Coole Nature Reserve Galway ... 25 P4
Coolfadda Galway ... 35 K9
Coolgreany/*Cúil Chréine* Wexfd ... 23 M1
Coolick Kerry ... 10 B5
Coolieragh Cork ... 3 Q4
Coolmore Cross Cork ... 6 E6
Coolnagun Wmeath ... 45 L9
Coolnasmear Watfd ... 13 M5
Coolock C Dubl ... 39 M6
Coolrain Cross Laois ... 28 G6
Coolyslin Lower Donegl ... 60 C4
Coolyslin Upper Donegl ... 60 C4
Coon/*Coan* Kilken ... 29 N10
Coonane Cork ... 4 B3
Coonnaluinga Galway ... 32 F1
Cooraclare/*Cuar an Chláir* Clare ... 17 J2
Coosane Tippry ... 19 K1
Cootehill/*Muinchille* Cavan ... 54 G10
Coppeen Cork ... 5 J2
Copperalley Cork ... 7 L3
Corbally Cross Laois ... 29 K7
Corbet AB & C ... 56 F4
Corclogh/*An Chorrchloch* Mayo ... 48 E4
Cork/*Corcaigh* C Cork ... 6 C4
Cork Airport Cork ... 6 C5
Corkey CC & G ... 68 B8
Corkley AB & C ... 55 N6
Corlismore Cavan ... 45 K4
Cornafean Cavan ... 45 K4
Cornamona/*Corr na Móna* Galway ... 33 L3
Cornelscourt Dublin ... 39 N8
Corrandromaun Crossroads Watfd ... 12 H7
Corr na Móna/*Cornamona* Galway ... 33 L3
Corrofin Galway ... 34 E5
Corrofin/*Cora Finne* Clare ... 25 L7
Costelloe/*Casla* Galway ... 33 K8
Courtbrack Cork ... 11 P9
Courtmacsherry/*Cúirt Mhic Shéafraidh* Cork ... 5 N6
Courtnacuddy Wexfd ... 22 F7
Courtown/*Baile na Cúirte* Wexfd ... 23 M3
Courtstown Cork ... 6 E4
Craanford Wexfd ... 23 K2
Craggaunowen Project Clare ... 26 C10
Craigavole CC & G ... 67 M10
Craigavon AB & C ... 56 C1
Cranagh D & S ... 61 J4
Cratloe Clare ... 18 F2
Craughwell/*Creachmhaoil* Galway ... 34 G9
Crawfordsburn A & ND ... 63 M6
Creagh Cork ... 4 D8
Creagh/*An Chríoch* Galway ... 35 P7
Crecora Limrck ... 18 G5
Creegh/*An Chríoch* Clare ... 17 J1
Creeslough/*An Craoslach* Donegl ... 65 K6
Creevy Donegl ... 58 H10
Creggan NM & D ... 55 P9
Creggs Galway ... 35 M1
Crettyard Laois ... 29 N9
Crinkill Offaly ... 28 C4
Croagh Limrck ... 18 E6
Croboy Meath ... 37 Q4
Croghan Offaly ... 37 M7
Croithlí/*Crolly* Donegl ... 64 E9
Croke Park/*Páirc an Chrócaigh* C Dubl ... 39 M6
Crolly/*Croithlí* Donegl ... 64 E9
Cromane/*An Cromán* Kerry ... 9 K5
Cronagort Clare ... 24 G5
Crookedwood/*Tigh Munna* Wmeath ... 37 M1
Crookedwood Cross Laois ... 29 J8
Crookhaven/*An Cruachán* Cork ... 3 N9

Crookstown Cork ... 5 L1
Crookstown Kildre ... 30 E5
Croom/*Cromadh* Limrck ... 18 G6
Crosreagh Cork ... 5 M5
Cross Mayo ... 33 P2
Crossabeg Wexfd ... 15 N3
Crossakeel/*Crosa Caoil* Meath ... 46 B9
Crossbarry Cork ... 5 P2
Cross Bridge Wicklw ... 31 J9
Crossdoney Cavan ... 45 L3
Crossgar NM & D ... 57 M2
Crosshaven/*Bun an Tábhairne* Cork ... 6 E6
Crosskeys/ Cavan ... 45 N4
Crossmaglen NM & D ... 55 P9
Crossmolina/*Crois Mhaoilíona* Mayo ... 50 D8
Crossnacole Bridge Wicklw ... 30 G8
Crossnacreevy L & C ... 63 K9
Crumlin A & N ... 62 F7
Crusheen/*Croisín* Clare ... 25 N7
Crushoa Galway ... 25 N2
Cuckel's Crossroads Kildre ... 30 D5
Cuddagh Cross Laois ... 28 H7
Culdaff/*Cúil Dabhcha* Donegl ... 66 E3
Cullahill Laois ... 29 J10
Cullaville NM & D ... 55 N10
Cullen Tippry ... 19 N6
Cullenstown/*Baile Uí Choileáin* Wexfd ... 15 K7
Cullybackey E Antr ... 62 D1
Cullyfad Longfd ... 44 G8
Cullyhanna NM & D ... 55 P8
Culmore D & S ... 66 D8
Culmullin Meath ... 38 G4
Curracloe Wexfd ... 15 P3
Curragha Meath ... 39 J2
Curraghavoe Cork ... 12 E2
Curraghboy Roscom ... 35 Q4
Curraghmore Cork ... 12 E2
Curragh Racecourse Kildre ... 30 D2
Curran M Ulst ... 61 Q3
Curry/*An Choraidh* Sligo ... 42 G2
Cushendall CC & G ... 68 E7
Cushendun CC & G ... 68 E6
Cut Bush Kildre ... 30 D3

D

Daingean/*An Daingean* Offaly ... 37 M8
Daingean Uí Chúis/*An Daingean/Dingle* Kerry ... 8 E4
Dalkey/*Deilginis* Dublin ... 39 P8
Darkley AB & C ... 55 N6
Darragh Limrck ... 12 B1
Darragh Cross NM & D ... 57 M1
Darver Louth ... 47 K4
Davidstown Wexfd ... 22 G7
Dawros Kerry ... 3 P1
Delgany/*Deilgne* Wicklw ... 31 P2
Delvin/*Dealbhna* Wmeath ... 37 Q1
Deputy's Pass Wicklw ... 31 N6
Dernacartha Roscom ... 43 J3
Dernaflaw CC & G ... 61 L1
Derraugh Cross Laois ... 29 J5
Derreentaggart Cork ... 3 K5
Derrinturn Kildre ... 38 C7
Derry/*Londonderry* D & S ... 66 C9
Derrybeg/*Doirí Beaga* Donegl ... 64 E7
Derryboye NM & D ... 57 M1
Derrybrien Galway ... 26 E4
Derrygonnelly F & O ... 53 M2
Derryhaun Longfd ... 36 D1
Derryheena Clare ... 25 P7
Derrykearn Cross Laois ... 29 K7
Derrykeighan CC & G ... 67 P6
Derryleigh Bridge Cork ... 4 F7
Derrylin F & O ... 53 Q7
Derrymacash AB & C ... 56 C1
Derrymore Kerry ... 8 G9
Derry Walls D & S ... 66 C9
Dervock CC & G ... 67 P6
Desertmartin M Ulst ... 61 Q4
Dickeystown A & N ... 62 H4
Dingle/*An Daingean/ Daingean Uí Chúis* Kerry ... 8 E4
Dingle Oceanworld Kerry ... 8 E4
Doagh A & N ... 62 H5
Doirí Beaga/*Derrybeg* Donegl ... 64 E7
Dolla Tippry ... 27 L10

Dollingstown AB & C ... 56 E1
Donabate/*Domhnach Bat* Dublin ... 39 N3
Donacarney Meath ... 47 M9
Donagh F & O ... 54 C7
Donaghadee A & ND ... 63 P7
Donaghcloney AB & C ... 56 E2
Donaghmore Laois ... 28 G8
Donaghmore M Ulst ... 61 N9
Donaghmore Meath ... 39 K3
Donaghmore Meath ... 46 G9
Donard/*Dún Ard* Wicklw ... 30 G5
Donaskeagh Tippry ... 19 Q6
Donegal/*Dún na nGall* Donegl ... 59 K7
Donegal Airport Donegl ... 64 D8
Donemana/ *Dunnamanagh* D & S ... 60 F2
Doneraile/*Dún ar Aill* Cork ... 11 Q3
Donohill Tippry ... 19 Q6
Donore Kildre ... 38 E9
Donore Meath ... 47 K9
Donoughmore Cork ... 11 M8
Dooagh Mayo ... 40 D3
Doocharry/*An Dúchoraidh* Donegl ... 59 J1
Dooega/*Dumha Éige* Mayo ... 40 E4
Doogary Roscom ... 43 K4
Doohamlet Monhan ... 55 L8
Doohat Bridge Monhan ... 54 G8
Doohooma/*Dumha Thuama* Mayo ... 48 F8
Doolin/*Dúlainn* Clare ... 24 G5
Doon Galway ... 35 L6
Doon Offaly ... 36 E7
Doon/*Dún* Limrck ... 19 N4
Doonbeg Clare ... 16 H1
Dooneen Clare ... 25 N9
Dooniver/*Dún Ibhir* Mayo ... 40 F2
Dooyork/*Dumha Dhearc* Mayo ... 48 F8
Douglas Cork ... 6 D5
Douglas Bridge D & S ... 60 E4
Downey's Bridge Cork ... 11 M8
Downhill Demesne & Hezlett House CC & G ... 67 K5
Downings/*Na Dúnaibh* Donegl ... 65 K5
Downpatrick NM & D ... 57 M4
Dowra Leitrm ... 53 J7
Doyle's Cross Laois ... 29 N8
Drains Bay E Antr ... 63 K1
Drangan/*Drongán* Tippry ... 20 H6
Draperstown M Ulst ... 61 N4
Drimoleague/*Drom dhá Liag* Cork ... 4 E5
Dripsey Cork ... 11 M10
Drogheda/*Droichead Átha* Louth ... 47 L8
Droichead Bhaile an tSléibhe/*Ballintlea Bridge* Watfd ... 13 M8
Droim Loch Druid/ *Drumlaghdrid* Donegl ... 58 G1
Drom Tippry ... 20 D1
Dromahair/*Droim Dhá Thair* Leitrm ... 52 F6
Dromara L & C ... 56 H3
Drombane Kerry ... 3 P2
Dromcollogher/*Drom Collachair* Limrck ... 18 D10
Dromina/*Drom Aidhne* Cork ... 11 M1
Dromineer Tippry ... 27 K7
Dromiskin Louth ... 47 L4
Dromkeen Limrck ... 19 L5
Drommahane Cork ... 11 N5
Drommartin Kerry ... 16 E8
Dromod/*Dromad* Leitrm ... 44 E6
Dromore AB & C ... 56 G2
Dromore F & O ... 60 D10
Dromore West Sligo ... 51 K5
Drumahoe D & S ... 66 D9
Drumaness NM & D ... 57 K3
Drumaroad NM & D ... 57 K4
Drumbane Tippry ... 20 C3
Drumbeg L & C ... 63 J9
Drumbo L & C ... 63 J9
Drumcliff/*Droim Chliabh* Sligo ... 52 C4
Drumcondra/*Droim Conrach* Meath ... 46 G6
Drumcree Wmeath ... 45 Q10
Drumdangan Wicklw ... 31 N6
Drumfries/*Droim Fraoigh* Donegl ... 66 B5
Drumgarra Monhan ... 55 L9
Drumkeen Donegl ... 59 Q2

Drumkeeran/*Droim Caorthainn* Leitrm ... 52 H8
Drumkilly Cavan ... 45 M5
Drumlaghdrid/*Droim Loch Druid* Donegl ... 58 G1
Drumlish/*Droim Lis* Longfd ... 44 G6
Drumquin F & O ... 60 D8
Drumree Meath ... 38 G3
Drumshallon Louth ... 47 L7
Drumshanbo/*Droim Seanbhó* Leitrm ... 44 C1
Drumsna/*Droim ar Snámh* Leitrm ... 44 C4
Drumsurn CC & G ... 67 J9
Drung Cavan ... 45 P1
Duagh/*Dubháth* Kerry ... 17 K8
Dualla Tippry ... 20 E6
Dublin/*Baile Átha Cliath* C Dubl ... 39 M7
Dublin Airport Dublin ... 39 M5
Dublin Castle C Dubl ... 39 M7
Dublin Zoo C Dubl ... 39 L6
Duggan's Hill Galway ... 27 J3
Dugort Mayo ... 40 E2
Duleek/*Damhliag* Meath ... 47 K10
Dumha Dhearc/*Dooyork* Mayo ... 48 F8
Dumha Éige/*Dooega* Mayo ... 40 E4
Dumha Thuama/ *Doohooma* Mayo ... 48 F8
Dunabrattin/*Dún an Bhratain* Watfd ... 14 B9
Dunadry A & N ... 62 F5
Dún Aonghasa Galway ... 24 B2
Dunbell Kilken ... 21 P4
Dunboyne/*Dún Búinne* Meath ... 39 J5
Duncannon/*Dún Canann* Wexfd ... 14 G7
Dún Chaoin/*Dunquin* Kerry ... 8 C4
Duncormick/*Dun Cormaic* Wexfd ... 15 L7
Dundalk/*Dún Dealgan* Louth ... 47 K2
Dunderrow Cork ... 5 P4
Dunderry Meath ... 38 E1
Dundonald L & C ... 63 L8
Dundrod L & C ... 62 G7
Dundrum Dublin ... 39 M8
Dundrum NM & D ... 57 L5
Dundrum Tippry ... 20 B5
Dunfanaghy/*Dún Fionnachaidh* Donegl ... 65 J5
Dungannon M Ulst ... 61 N10
Dungarvan Kilken ... 21 Q5
Dungarvan/*Dún Garbhán* Watfd ... 13 N6
Dungiven CC & G ... 61 L1
Dungiven Priory CC & G ... 61 L1
Dungloe/*Dunglow/An Clochán Liath* Donegl ... 64 D10
Dunglow/*An Clochán Liath* Donegl ... 64 D10
Dungourney Cork ... 6 H3
Dunhill Watfd ... 14 C8
Dún Ibhir/*Dooniver* Mayo ... 40 F2
Dunkineely/*Dún Cionnaola* Donegl ... 58 G7
Dún Laoghaire Dublin ... 39 N8
Dunlavin/*Dún Luáin* Wicklw ... 30 F4
Dunleer/*Dún Léire* Louth ... 47 L6
Dunloy CC & G ... 67 Q9
Dunmanway/ *Dúnmaonmhuí* Cork ... 4 G4
Dunmore/*Dún Mhór* Kilken ... 21 N2
Dunmore/*Dún Mór* Galway ... 34 G1
Dunmore East/*Dún Mór* Watfd ... 14 F8
Dunmurry Belfst ... 62 H9
Dunnamaggan Kilken ... 21 M7
Dunnamanagh/ *Donemana* D & S ... 60 F2
Dunquin/*Dún Chaoin* Kerry ... 8 C4
Dunsany/*Dún Samhna* Meath ... 38 G2
Dunseverick CC & G ... 67 P4
Dunshaughlin/*Dún Seachlainn* Meath ... 38 H3
Durrow Offaly ... 37 J7
Durrow/*Darú* Laois ... 29 K9
Durrus/*Dúrras* Cork ... 3 Q6
Dursey Island Cork ... 2 F6

Dysart/*An Díseart* Roscom .. 35   P4
Dysart Cross Laois.............. 29   L8

E

Eadestown Kildre............... 38   G10
Easky/*Iascaigh* Sligo 51   J4
Edenderry/*Éaden Doire*
   Offaly 37   Q7
Edenfinfreagh/*An*
   tÉaden Anfach Donegl...... 59   J4
Ederney F & O.................. 60   B10
Edgeworthstown/
   Meathas Troim Longfd.... 45   J9
Effin Limrck..................... 18   H10
Eglinton D & S.................. 66   E8
Eglish M Ulst.................... 55   L1
Elphin/*Ail Finn* Roscom 43   Q6
Elton Limrck..................... 19   K8
Emly/*Imleach* Tippry......... 19   M8
Emo Laois........................ 29   M3
Emyvale/*Scairbh na*
   gCaorach Monhan 55   J4
Enfield/*An Bóthar Buí*
   Meath 38   D5
Enfield Services Kildre........ 38   C5
Ennis/*Inis* Clare 25   M9
Enniscorthy/*Inis*
   Córthaidh Wexfd 22   H7
Enniscrone/*Inishcrone/*
   Inis Crabhann Sligo....... 50   G6
Enniskean/*Inis Céin* Cork... 5   K4
Enniskerry/*Áth na Sceire*
   Wicklw......................... 31   N1
Enniskillen F & O............... 53   P4
Enniskillen Castle F & O.... 53   P4
Ennistymon/*Ennistimon/*
   Inis Díomáin Clare........ 24   H7
Ennybegs Longfd............... 44   G7
Errew Mayo...................... 41   Q7
Errill Laois...................... 28   F9
Eskavaud Cork 2   H5
Eskerbreague Offaly.......... 36   E7
Eyeries/*Na hAoraí* Cork 3   J4
Eyrecourt/*Dún an Uchta*
   Galway......................... 27   M1

F

Faha Galway 35   J7
Fahan/*Fathain* Donegl 65   Q7
Fahy Mayo....................... 41   M6
Falcarragh/*An Fál Carrach*
   Donegl.......................... 64   G6
Fanore/*Fánóir* Clare 24   H3
Farmleigh House Dublin 39   K6
Farran Cork 5   K8
Farran Cork 5   L5
Farran Cork 5   M1
Farran Cork 11   N7
Farran Cork 12   D6
Farranfore/*An Fearann*
   Fuar Kerry 9   Q4
Farravaun Galway 34   F6
Feakle/*An Fhiacail* Clare ... 26   E7
Fedamore/*Feadamair*
   Limrck.......................... 18   H6
Feenagh Limrck................ 18   E9
Feeny CC & G................... 61   K1
Fenit/*An Fhianait* Kerry..... 9   L1
Fennagh Carlow 22   D2
Fennor Watfd................... 14   C8
Ferbane/*An Féar Bán*
   Offaly........................... 36   E9
Fermoy/*Mainistir Fhear*
   Maí Cork..................... 12   D5
Ferns/*Fearna* Wexfd 23   J5
Fertagh Bridge Kilken 28   H10
Fethard/*Fiodh Ard* Tippry... 20   G7
Fethard/*Fiodh Ard* Wexfd ... 14   H7
Fews Watfd...................... 13   Q3
Fiddown/*Fiodh Dúin*
   Kilken........................... 21   M10
Fieries Kerry.................... 9   Q4
Finglas C Dubl.................. 39   L6
Fintona F & O.................... 60   F10
Fintown/*Baile na Finne*
   Donegl.......................... 59   K2
Finvoy CC & G................... 67   P9
Fionntrá/*Ventry* Kerry....... 8   D4
Fisherstown/*Baile*
   Fearainn Laois............. 29   P3
Fivemiletown M Ulst.......... 54   D3
Florence Court F & O....... 53   N4
Foher Cork 2   H6
Foreglen CC & G................ 61   K1
Forkhill NM & D................ 56   C9

Fossa/*An Fosadh* Kerry 9   Q6
Fota Wildlife Park Cork 6   E4
Foulkesmill Wexfd 15   K5
Fourmileburn A & N........... 62   G5
Fourmilewater Watfd 13   L2
Four Roads Roscom 35   P3
Foxford/*Béal Easa* Mayo.... 42   C3
Foxhole Cork 7   L3
Foynes/*Faing* Limrck 17   N4
Freemount/*Cillin an*
   Chrónáin Cork............. 11   K2
Frenchpark/*Dún Gar*
   Roscom........................ 43   M5
Freshford/*Achadh Úr*
   Kilken........................... 21   L2
Freyne's Bridghe Kildre 38   F7
Frosses/*Na Frosa* Donegl ... 58   H6
Fruit Hill Watfd................. 13   N5
Furbogh/*Na Forbacha*
   Galway......................... 33   P9
Furkeal Cork 3   Q4
Furrow Cork 12   E2

G

Galbally Wexfd................. 15   L3
Galbally/*An Gallbhaile*
   Limrck.......................... 19   M9
Galgorm E Antr................. 62   D2
Gallony CC & G 61   K1
Galway/*Gaillimh* C Gal 34   B8
Galway Atlantaquaria
   C Gal........................... 34   B9
Galway City Museum
   C Gal........................... 34   B9
Galway Services Galway 34   H9
Gaoth Dobhair/
   Gweedore Donegl 64   F8
Gaoth Sáile/*Gweesalia*
   Mayo........................... 48   G7
Garbally Offaly................. 36   G10
Garmna/*Gorumna Island*
   Galway......................... 32   H9
Garrafrauns Galway 42   G10
Garrans Cross Laois.......... 29   N5
Garraun Cross Laois.......... 29   K9
Garrison F & O.................. 52   H2
Garristown Dublin............ 39   K2
Garryduff Cork 11   L4
Garrykennedy Tippry......... 27   J8
Garrymore Offaly.............. 36   B9
Garrynageragh Watfd........ 13   N6
Garryspillane Limrck......... 19   L9
Garryvoe Cork 7   J5
Garvagh CC & G 67   L9
Garvagh Leitrm................ 44   E3
Garvary F & O................... 53   Q3
Garvetagh D & S............... 60   C6
Geashill/*Géisill* Offaly..... 37   M9
Geneva Cross Laois........... 29   N9
George Best Belfast City
   Airport Belfst.............. 63   K7
Giant's Causeway CC & G.... 67   N4
Gilford AB & C.................. 56   D3
Gilroe Galway................... 26   C6
Glandore/*Cúan Dor* Cork 4   G7
Glangevlin Cavan.............. 53   L7
Glanmire/*Gleann Maghair*
   Cork............................ 6   D4
Glanshanacuirp/*Gleann*
   Seandhoirp Kerry 8   F3
Glansheskin Cork 12   D4
Glanworth/*Gleannúir*
   Cork............................ 12   C4
Glarryford E Antr 68   B10
Glaslough/*Glasloch*
   Monhan 55   K4
Glassamucky Dublin 39   L9
Glassan/*Glasán* Wmeath... 36   D4
Glastry A & ND 63   Q10
Gleann Cholm Cille/
   Glencolumbkille Donegl 58   B6
Gleann na Muaidhe/
   Glenamoy Mayo 49   J5
Gleann Seandhoirp/
   Glanshanacuirp Kerry..... 8   F3
Glen Donegl..................... 65   L6
Glen Donegl..................... 65   N8
Glen Donegl..................... 66   C8
Glenamaddy/*Gleann na*
   Madadh Galway........... 35   J1
Glenamoy/*Gleann na*
   Muaidhe Mayo 49   J5
Glenarm E Antr................ 68   G9
Glenavy L & C................... 62   F8
Glenbeigh/*Gleann Beithe*
   Kerry........................... 9   K6
Glenbrien Wexfd 23   J7

Glenbrook Cork................ 6   E5
Glencar Kerry................... 9   L8
Glencolumbkille/*Gleann*
   Cholm Cille Donegl........ 58   B6
Glencoria Wicklw.............. 31   M5
Glencullen/*Gleann*
   Cuilinn Dublin............. 39   M9
Glendalough/*Gleann Dá*
   Loch Wicklw................ 31   L5
Glendalough Monastic
   Site Wicklw................... 31   L5
Glenealy/*Gleann Fhaidhle*
   Wicklw......................... 31   N6
Gleneely Donegl............... 66   E4
Glengarriff/*An Gleann*
   Garbh Cork.................. 3   Q3
Glenisland Mayo............... 41   N4
Glenmalure Wicklw........... 31   L6
Glenoe E Antr................... 63   K3
Glenroe Limrck................. 12   B1
Glenties/*Na Gleannta*
   Donegl.......................... 58   H4
Glenveagh National Park
   Donegl.......................... 65   J9
Glenville/*Gleann an*
   Phréacháin Cork........... 12   B7
Glin/*An Gleann* Limrck 17   L5
Glounthaune Cork 6   E4
Glynn Carlow................... 22   C7
Glynn E Antr.................... 63   L3
Glynn Wexfd.................... 15   M3
Goatanbridge Tippry......... 13   J2
Goatstown Dublin............ 39   M8
Gob an Choire/*Achill*
   Sound Mayo................ 40   F4
Goggins Hill Cork............. 5   Q2
Golden/*An Gabhailin*
   Tippry.......................... 20   C7
Goleen Cork 3   N9
Goresbridge/*An*
   Droichead Nua Kilken...... 22   B4
Gorey/*Guaire* Wexfd......... 23   M3
Gorey Services Wexfd........ 23   N1
Gormanstown Meath......... 47   N10
Gort/*Gort Inse Guaire*
   Galway......................... 26   C4
Gortaghig Cork................ 2   H5
Gortahork/*Gort an*
   Choirce Donegl............ 64   G6
Gort an Choirce/
   Gortahork Donegl......... 64   G6
Gortbreagoge Kerry 9   J4
Gorteen Sligo.................. 43   L2
Gortin F & O.................... 60   G5
Gortletteragh Leitrm........ 44   F5
Gortlicka Kerry................ 3   P1
Gortnaclohy Cork............. 4   E8
Gortnahultra Galway......... 35   J6
Gortnakilla Kerry.............. 10   D8
Gortnaskehy Cork............ 12   F3
Gortroe Cork 4   B3
Gortroe Kerry.................. 9   Q6
Gorumna Island/*Garmna*
   Galway......................... 32   H9
Gougane Barra/*Guagán*
   Barra Cork.................. 4   D1
Gour Cork 3   J6
Gowna Cavan................... 45   K5
Gowran/*Gabhrán* Kilken.... 21   Q4
Gracehill E Antr 62   D2
Graham's Cross Laois........ 29   P9
Graig Cork 11   R2
Graigue Cross Laois.......... 29   M7
Graiguenamanagh/*Gráig*
   na Manach Kilken.......... 22   C6
Granard/*Gránard* Longfd... 45   K7
Grange Kilken................... 21   M4
Grange Louth................... 47   N2
Grange Tippry.................. 21   J3
Grange/*An Ghráinseach*
   Sligo........................... 52   C3
Grangebellew Louth.......... 47   L6
Grangeford Bridge Kildre ... 30   D7
Granville M Ulst............... 61   N10
Greencastle Donegl.......... 66   H4
Greencastle F & O............ 61   J6
Greenisland E Antr........... 63   K5
Greenore/*An Grianfort*
   Louth........................... 47   P1
Gregory's Cross Roads
   Laois........................... 29   P8
Grenagh Cork 11   P8
Greyabbey A & ND 63   P9
Greysteel CC & G 66   F8
Greystones/*Na Clocha*
   Liatha Wicklw.............. 31   P2
Groomsport A & ND 63   N6
Guagán Barra/*Gougane*
   Barra Cork.................. 4   D1

Gulladuff M Ulst............... 61   Q3
Gun Point Cork................. 3   P9
Gurteen Galway................ 35   J6
Gurteen Leitrm................ 52   E4
Gurteens Mayo................. 50   F8
Gusserane Wexfd.............. 14   H5
Gweedore/*Gaoth Dobhair*
   Donegl.......................... 64   F8
Gweesalia/*Gaoth Sáile*
   Mayo........................... 48   G7
Gyles Quay Louth.............. 47   N2

H

Hacketstown/*Baile*
   Haicéid Carlow 30   H8
Halfway Cork.................... 5   Q2
Hamiltons Bawn AB & C...... 55   P4
Hammondstown Louth 47   K6
Harestown Louth.............. 47   L7
Harristown Kildre............. 30   B3
Hawksford Roscom........... 43   J4
Headford/*Áth Cinn* Galway ... 34   B4
Helen's Bay A & ND........... 63   M6
Hell Kettle Bridge Wicklw... 30   C5
Hennebry's Cross Kilken 21   M2
Herbertstown/*Baile*
   Hiobaird Limrck........... 19   K6
Hillhall L & C.................... 62   H10
Hill of Tara Meath............. 38   G2
Hillsborough L & C............ 56   G1
Hilltown Donegl................ 58   G6
Hilltown NM & D............... 56   G7
Hilltown Wexfd................. 15   K6
Hollyford Tippry............... 19   Q4
Hollyfort Wexfd................ 23   L2
Hollymount Mayo.............. 42   C10
Hollywood/*Cillin*
   Chaoimhín Wicklw........ 30   G3
Holycross Limrck.............. 19   J7
Holycross Tippry............... 20   D4
Holycross Abbey Tippry 20   D4
Holywood A & ND............. 63   L7
Horse and Jockey Tippry 20   F4
Horseleap Wmeath............ 36   H6
Hospital/*An tOspidéal*
   Limrck.......................... 19   L7
Howth/*Binn Éadair* Dublin... 39   P6
Hugginstown Kilken........... 21   N8
Huntsman Cross Carlow...... 22   D1

I

Inagh/*Eidhneach* Clare 25   K8
Inch Kerry....................... 9   J4
Inch/*An Inis* Wexfd........... 23   M1
Inches Cork 3   K5
Inchicloon Kerry............... 3   P1
Inchigeelagh/*Inse*
   Geimhleach Cork.......... 4   G1
Inchinattin Cross Roads
   Cork............................ 4   H6
Inchintaggart Cork............ 3   Q3
Inis Bó Finne/*Inishbofin*
   Galway......................... 40   B10
Inis Crabhann/
   Inishcrone/Enniscrone
   Sligo........................... 50   G6
Inishbofin/*Inis Bó Finne*
   Galway......................... 40   B10
Inishcrone/*Enniscrone/*
   Inis Crabhann Sligo....... 50   G6
Inisheer/*Inis Oírr* Galway... 24   E4
Inishmaan/*Inis Meáin*
   Galway......................... 24   D4
Inishmore/*Inis Mór* Galway ... 24   B3
Inishowen Donegl............. 66   C4
Inishturk/*Inis Toirc* Mayo... 40   D9
Inis Meáin/*Inishmaan*
   Galway......................... 24   D4
Inis Mór/*Inishmore* Galway ... 24   B3
Inis Oírr/*Inisheer* Galway... 24   E4
Inistioge/*Inis Tíog* Kilken... 21   Q7
Inis Toirc/*Inishturk* Mayo... 40   D9
Innishannon/*Inis Eonáin*
   Cork............................ 5   N3
Inniskeen/*Inis Caoin*
   Monhan 46   H2
Innisrush M Ulst............... 62   A2
Inver/*Inbhear* Donegl....... 58   H7
Ireland West Airport
   Knock Mayo................ 42   G4
Irish National Stud &
   Japanese Gardens Kildre... 30   C2
Irishtown Mayo................ 42   F10
Irvinestown F & O............. 53   P1
Iscaheen Donegl............... 66   D7

Islandmagee E Antr 63 M3
Iveragh Peninsula/*Uibh*
Ráthach Kerry 8 F7

J

Jameson Experience Cork 6 G4
Jenkinstown Kilken 21 M1
Jerpoint Abbey Kilken 21 P6
Jerrettspass NM & D 56 D6
John F Kennedy
Arboretum Wexfd 14 G5
Johnstown Cork 4 H2
Johnstown Meath 46 G10
Johnstown Wicklw 30 H3
Johnstown/*Baile Eoin*
Kildre 38 G9
Johnstown/*Baile Sheáin*
Kilken 20 H1
Johns Well Kilken 21 P2
Jonesborough NM & D........ 56 D9
Julianstown Meath 47 M10
Junction 14 Mayfield
Services Kildre 29 Q2

K

Kanturk/*Ceann Toirc* Cork ... 11 K4
Keadue/*Céideadh*
Roscom 44 B1
Keady AB & C 55 M6
Kealkill Cork 4 C3
Keane's Crossroads Cork 12 E3
Keating's Cross Laois 29 N7
Keel/*An Caol* Mayo 40 D3
Keelbanada Roscom 43 L4
Keeloges Mayo 42 B5
Kells E Antr 62 E3
Kells Kerry 8 H7
Kells/*Ceanannas* Kilken 21 M6
Kells/*Ceanannas* Meath 46 D8
Kelly's Cross Laois 29 K8
Kellyville Laois 29 P6
Kenagh/*Caonach* Longfd 36 E1
Kenmare/*Neidín* Kerry 9 Q10
Kentstown Meath 47 J10
Kerry Airport Kerry 10 B4
Kerrykeel/*An Cheathrú*
Chaol Donegl 65 N6
Kerry Pike Cork 11 Q10
Kesh F & O 59 Q10
Keshcarrigan Leitrm 44 D2
Kielduff Kerry 9 Q1
Kilanerin Wexfd 23 M1
Kilbaha Clare 16 C5
Kilbeggan/*Cill Bheagáin*
Wmeath 37 J6
Kilbehenny Limrck 12 E1
Kilberry Kildre 29 Q5
Kilberry Meath 46 G9
Kilbraghan/*Cill*
Bhearcháin Kilken 21 K5
Kilbride Meath 39 K4
Kilbrien Watfd 13 M4
Kilbrin/*Cill Bhrain* Cork 11 L3
Kilbrittain/*Cill Briotáin*
Cork 5 N5
Kilcar/*Cill Charthaigh*
Donegl 58 D7
Kilcatherine Cork 3 J4
Kilchreest/*Cill Chríost*
Galway 26 E2
Kilclief NM & D 57 P3
Kilclogh Cork 12 D4
Kilclone/*Coill Chluana*
Meath 38 G5
Kilcloon/*Chill Chluana*
Meath 38 G5
Kilcock/*Cill Choca* Meath ... 38 F6
Kilcogy Cavan 45 L6
Kilcolgan/*Cill Cholgáin*
Galway 34 E10
Kilcolman Limrck 17 P6
Kilconly Galway 34 D2
Kilconnell Galway 35 L7
Kilcoo NM & D 56 H6
Kilcoole/*Cill Chomhghaill*
Wicklw 31 P3
Kilcormac/*Cill Chormaic*
Offaly 28 E2
Kilcrohane Cork 3 N7
Kilcullen/*Cill Chuillinn*
Kildre 30 E3
Kilcummin Kerry 8 H2
Kilcummin Kerry 10 B5
Kilcurly Louth 47 K2
Kildalkey Meath 38 C2

Kildangan Kildre 29 Q3
Kildare/*Cill Dara* Kildre........ 30 C2
Kildavin Carlow 22 F2
Kildoney Donegl 60 B3
Kildoon Kildre 30 C3
Kildorrery/*Cill Dairbhre*
Cork 12 B2
Kildrum Cork 12 E2
Kildrum Donegl 66 B10
Kilfenora/*Cill*
Fhionnúrach Clare 25 J6
Kilfinane/*Cill Fhíonáin*
Limrck 19 K10
Kilflynn Kerry 16 F10
Kilgarvan/*Cill Garbháin*
Kerry 10 C10
Kilgobnet Watfd 13 M5
Kilkea/*Cill Cathaigh* Kildre.... 30 C7
Kilkee/*Cill Chaoi* Clare 16 F3
Kilkeel NM & D 57 J10
Kilkelly/*Cill Cheallaigh*
Mayo 42 F5
Kilkenny/*Cill Chainnigh*
Kilken 21 N3
Kilkenny Castle Kilken 21 N3
Kilkieran/*Cill Chiaráin*
Galway 32 G7
Kilkishen/*Cill Chisín* Clare ... 26 C10
Kill Cavan 45 Q2
Kill Watfd 14 B8
Kill/*An Chill* Kildre 38 G9
Killadysert Clare 17 P3
Killaha East Kerry 3 Q1
Killala/*Cill Ala* Mayo 50 F5
Killaloe Clare 26 H10
Killaloo D & S 60 H1
Killan Galway 35 L3
Killanena Clare 26 D6
Killann/*Cill Anna* Wexfd 22 F6
Killaphort Offaly 36 B9
Killarga/*Cill Fhearga*
Leitrm 52 G6
Killarney/*Cill Airne* Kerry 10 B6
Killarney National Park
Kerry 10 B9
Killashandra/*Cill na*
Seanrátha Cavan 45 K2
Killashee Longfd 44 E9
Killasmeestia Laois............ 28 F8
Killavullen/*Cill an*
Mhuilinn Cork 11 Q5
Killawalla Mayo 41 N8
Killea D & S 66 B10
Killea Leitrm 52 H4
Killea Tippry 28 C10
Killea Watfd 14 F8
Killead A & N 62 F7
Killeagh/*Cill Ia* Cork 7 K3
Killeen Galway 26 C6
Killeen Laois 30 B8
Killeen Mayo 40 G8
Killeevan Monhan 54 G7
Killeigh/*Cill Aichidh* Offaly..... 37 K10
Killen D & S 60 B7
Killenard Laois 29 N3
Killenaule/*Cill Náile* Tippry 20 G5
Killeshin Laois 30 B9
Killeter D & S 60 B6
Killimer Clare 17 K4
Killimor/*Cill Íomair* Galway 27 K2
Killina Offaly 36 H9
Killinaboy/*Cill Iníne*
Baoith Clare 25 L6
Killinchy A & ND 63 N10
Killiney/*Cill Iníon Léinín*
Dublin 39 P8
Killinick Wexfd 15 P6
Killinkere Cavan 46 B5
Killorglin/*Cill Orglan* Kerry 9 M5
Killough Cork 2 H6
Killough NM & D 57 N5
Killowen NM & D 56 F9
Killucan/*Cill Liúcainne*
Wmeath 37 P3
Killult/*Cill Ulta* Donegl 64 G6
Killurin Offaly 37 J10
Killurin Wexfd 15 M3
Killybegs/*Na Cealla Beaga*
Donegl 58 F7
Killydoon Cavan 45 L5
Killyfaddy AB & C 55 N5
Killygordon/*Cúil na*
gCuirridín Donegl 60 B4
Killylea AB & C 55 L3
Killyleagh NM & D 57 N2
Killyon Offaly 28 D3
Killyrammer CC & G 67 P7
Kilmacanogue/*Cill*
Mocheanóg Wicklw 31 N2

Kilmacow/*Cill Mhic*
Bhúith Kilken 14 D5
Kilmacrenan/*Cill Mhic*
Réanáin Donegl 65 L8
Kilmacthomas/*Coill Mhic*
Thomáisín Watfd 13 Q3
Kilmaganny/*Cill*
Mogeanna Kilken 21 M8
Kilmaine Mayo 34 B2
Kilmainham Gaol C Dubl 39 L7
Kilmainham Wood Meath.... 46 E6
Kilmaley Clare 25 K9
Kilmallock/*Cill*
Mocheallóg Limrck 19 J9
Kilmanagh/*Cill Mhanach*
Kilken 21 K4
Kilmead/*Cill Míde* Kildre...... 30 C5
Kilmeadan Watfd 14 C7
Kilmeage/*Cill Maodhóg*
Kildre 38 D9
Kilmeedy/*Cill Míde* Limrck ... 18 D9
Kilmessan Meath 38 F2
Kilmichael Cork 4 H1
Kilmihil/*Cill Mhichíl* Clare..... 17 L2
Kilmore AB & C 55 P2
Kilmore Mayo 42 C3
Kilmore NM & D 57 L2
Kilmore/*An Chill Mhór*
Wexfd 15 M7
Kilmore Quay/*Cé na Cille*
Móire Wexfd 15 M8
Kilmovee Mayo 42 H5
Kilmoyly Kerry 16 D9
Kilmuckridge/*Cill*
Mhucraise Wexfd 23 M6
Kilmurray Cork 5 K1
Kilmurry Clare 24 F10
Kilmurry Limrck 19 K9
Kilmurry Wicklw 30 G7
Kilmurry/*Cill Mhuire*
Clare 18 F1
Kilmyshall Wexfd 22 G4
Kilnafrehan Watfd 13 N5
Kilnaleck/*Cill na Leice*
Cavan 45 M5
Kilnamona Clare 25 L8
Kilpedder/*Cill Pheadair*
Wicklw 31 P3
Kilquade/*Cill Chomhaid*
Wicklw 31 P3
Kilraghts CC & G 67 Q7
Kilrane Wexfd 15 Q6
Kilrea CC & G 67 N10
Kilreekill/*Cill Ricill* Galway 35 K9
Kilronan/*Cill Rónáin*
Galway 24 C3
Kilross Tippry 19 N8
Kilruane Tippry 27 M8
Kilrush/*Cill Rois* Clare 16 H3
Kilsaran Louth 47 L5
Kilshane Cross Dublin 39 L5
Kilshannig Kerry 9 J1
Kilsheelan Tippry 20 H10
Kilskeery F & O 53 Q2
Kilskyre Meath 46 C9
Kiltannon Clare 26 C6
Kiltealy/*Cill Téile* Wexfd 22 F5
Kilteel Kildre 38 H9
Kilteely/*Cill Tile* Limrck 19 L6
Kiltegan Wicklw 30 G8
Kiltegan Bridge Wicklw 30 G8
Kilternan Dublin 39 N9
Kiltimagh/*Coillte Mách*
Mayo 42 D6
Kiltormer/*Cill Tormóir*
Galway 35 N9
Kiltyclogher/*Coillte*
Clochair Leitrm 53 J3
Kilwaughter E Antr 63 K2
Kilworth/*Cill Uird* Cork........ 12 D4
Kinallen AB & C 56 H3
Kinawley F & O 53 P6
Kincaslough/*Cionn*
Caslach Donegl 64 C9
King John's Castle Limrck 18 H3
Kingscourt/*Dún an Rí*
Cavan 46 E4
Kinlough/*Cionn Locha*
Leitrm 52 F1
Kinnegad/*Cionn Átha*
Gad Wmeath 37 P4
Kinnitty/*Cionn Eitigh*
Offaly 28 E3
Kinsale/*Cionn tSáile* Cork 6 B8
Kinvarra/*Cinn Mhara*
Galway 25 N2
Kircubbin A & ND 63 P10
Kirkistown A & ND 57 Q1
Kiskeam Cork 10 G4

Knappagh/*An Chnapach*
Mayo 41 L7
Knightstown Kerry 8 E9
Knock Clare 17 K4
Knock Tippry 28 F7
Knock/*Cnoc Mhuire* Mayo ... 42 E7
Knockaderry Limrck 18 C7
Knockadireen Kerry 17 J9
Knockainey/*Cnoc Áine*
Limrck 19 K7
Knockalougha Kerry 17 J9
Knockananna Wicklw 31 J8
Knockanean Clare 25 N9
Knockanteedan Dublin 39 K9
Knockaroe Laois 28 G7
Knockawaddra West
Kerry 9 P1
Knockbrack Galway 34 G7
Knockbracken L & C 63 K9
Knockbridge/*Droichead*
an Chnoic Louth 47 J3
Knockcarren Limrck 19 M8
Knockcloghrim M Ulst........ 61 Q3
Knockcroghery/*Cnoc an*
Chrochaire Roscom 35 Q2
Knockduff Kerry 3 Q2
Knockgour Cork 3 J6
Knocklong Limrck 19 L8
Knockmahon Watfd 14 A9
Knockmore Mayo 42 B2
Knocknacally Cork 7 L3
Knocknacarry CC & G 68 E6
Knocknagashel Kerry 17 K10
Knocknalina/*Cnocán na*
Líne Mayo 48 G4
Knockraha Cork 6 E3
Knockroe Cork 2 H6
Knocktopher/*Cnoc an*
Tóchair Kilken 21 N7
Kylemore Galway 27 J3

L

Labasheeda Clare 17 M4
Lack F & O 60 C9
Lackagh Galway 34 E6
Lacken Wicklw 31 J2
Ladysbridge Cork 7 J4
Lagavooren Meath 47 L9
Laghy/*An Lathaigh* Donegl 59 K8
Laharan Kerry 9 P1
Lahardane Mayo 41 P2
Lahinch/*Leacht Uí*
Chonchubhair Clare 24 G7
Lanesborough/*Béal Átha*
Liag Longfd 44 D10
Laragh Kildre 38 F6
Laragh Monhan 46 E1
Laragh/*An Laithreach*
Wicklw 31 L5
Larah Cavan 45 P2
Larchfield Cross Laois 29 L7
Largy Donegl 58 E7
Larkin's Cross Laois 29 M8
Larne E Antr 63 L2
Larry Cross Laois 28 H7
Lattin Tippry 19 N7
Lauragh/*An Láithreach*
Kerry 3 M3
Laurelvale AB & C 56 C3
Laurencetown/*An Baile*
Mór Galway 35 P9
Lavey/*Leamhaí* Cavan 45 P3
Lawrencetown AB & C 56 D3
Laytown/*An Inse* Meath 47 N9
Leabeg Offaly 36 F8
Leaby Cross Louth 47 J7
Leap/*An Léim* Cork 4 G7
Lecanvey/*Leac an Anfa*
Mayo 41 J7
Leckemy Donegl 66 F4
Leenaun/*Lionán* Galway 32 H1
Legan Longfd 36 G1
Legga Longfd 44 H5
Leighlinbridge/
Leithghlinn an Droichid
Carlow 22 B1
Leitir Mhic an Bhaird/
Lettermacaward Donegl.... 58 G2
Leitir Móir/*Lettermore*
Galway 32 H8
Leitreach Ard/*Letterard*
Galway 32 F6
Leitrim/*Liatroim* Leitrm 44 C3
Leixlip Kildre 39 J6
Lemanaghan Offaly 36 F8
Lemybrien Watfd 13 P4
Lenaderg AB & C 56 E3

Letterard/*Leitreach Ard*
Galway 32   F6
Letterbreen F & O 53   N4
Letterfrack/*Leitir Fraic*
Galway 32   E2
Letterkenny/*Leitir*
Ceanainn Donegl 65 M10
Lettermacaward/*Leitir*
Mhic an Bhaird Donegl .. 58   G2
Lettermore/*Leitir Móir*
Galway 32   H8
Lickbarrahane Cork 3   J6
Lifford/*Leifear* Donegl...... 60   D3
Limavady CC & G 66   H8
Limerick/*Luimneach*
Limrck 18   H3
Limerick City Gallery of
Art Limrck 18   H3
Limerick Junction Tippry ... 19   P7
Lisacul Roscom 43   J5
Lisbane A & ND 63 M10
Lisbellaw F & O 54   B4
Lisburn L & C 62 H10
Lisburn Services L & C 62   H9
Liscannor/*Lios Ceannúir*
Clare 24   G7
Liscarney/*Lios Cearnaigh*
Mayo 41   L8
Liscarroll/*Lios Cearúill*
Cork 11   M2
Lisdoonvarna/*Lios Dúin*
Bhearna Clare 24   H5
Lisgoold Cork 6   G2
Lismcaffrey Wmeath 45   L9
Lismonaghan Donegl 59   Q1
Lismore Kerry 9   P1
Lismore/*Lios Mór* Watfd .. 12   H5
Lismoyny Wmeath 36   H7
Lismulleyduff Donegl 59   Q5
Lisnagunnion Monhan 46   F2
Lisnamoyle Monhan 46   G2
Lisnarrick F & O 53   N1
Lisnaskea F & O 54   C6
Lisronagh Tippry 20   G9
Lisryan Longfd 45   K8
Lisselton Cross Kerry 16   L2
Lissycasey Clare 17   N1
Listack Donegl 59   P1
Listowel/*Lios Tuathail*
Kerry 16   H8
Lisvarrinane Tippry 19   N9
Little Island Cork 6   E4
Littleton/*An Baile Beag*
Tippry 20   F4
Lixnaw/*Leic Snámha*
Kerry 16   F9
Lochan Iúir/*Loughanure*
Donegl 64   E9
Loch Coirib/*Lough Corrib*
Galway 33   N4
Loch Measca/*Lough Mask*
Mayo 33   N1
Lombardstown Cork 11   M5
Londonderry/*Derry* D & S.. 66   C9
Longford Offaly 28   E4
Longford/*An Longfort*
Longfd 44   F8
Longford Cross Laois 28   C3
Longwood Meath 38   C4
Lorrha/*Lothra* Tippry 27   M4
Lough Clare 24   G6
Loughananna Limrck 12   E1
Loughanure/*Lochan Iúir*
Donegl 64   E9
Loughbrickland AB & C 56   E4
Lough Corrib/*Loch Coirib*
Galway 33   N4
Loughcrew Cairns Meath .. 45   Q8
Lough Derg Tippry 26   H8
Loughduff Cavan 45   L5
Lough Foyle CC & G 66   F7
Loughgall AB & C 55   P2
Loughglinn/*Loch Glinne*
Roscom 43   K6
Loughguile CC & G 68   B7
Lough Hill Clare 26   H6
Lough Mask/*Loch Measca*
Mayo 33   N1
Loughmore Tippry 20   E1
Loughnanemore Cork 2   G6
Loughnavalley Wmeath 37   J4
Lough Neagh A & N 62   C7
Loughrea/*Baile Locha*
Riach Galway 26   F1
Lough Ree Roscom 36   C3
Loughshinny/*Loch*
Sionnach Dublin 39   P2
Louisburgh/*Cluain*
Cearbán Mayo 40   H7

Louis Mulcahy Pottery
Kerry 8   C4
Louth/*Lú* Louth 47   J3
Lower Ballinderry L & C ... 62   E9
Lower Lough Erne F & O ... 53   M1
Lucan Dublin 39   J6
Lumville Cross Kildre 30   D2
Lurgan AB & C 56   D1
Lurgankiel Louth 47   K1
Lusk/*Lusca* Dublin 39   N3
Lusk Services Dublin 39   M2
Lyracrumpane Kerry 16 H10
Lyre Cork 5   K5
Lyre Cork 11   L6
Lyre Cork 12   G7
Lyre Kerry 10   D2

M

Maam Cross/*An Teach*
Dóite Galway 33   K4
Machaire Rabhartaigh/
Magheraroarty Donegl 64   F6
Macosquin CC & G 67   L7
Macroney Cork 12   E4
Macroom/*Maigh*
Chromtha Cork 11 J10
Maghaberry L & C 62 F10
Maghera Cavan 46   B7
Maghera M Ulst 61   Q2
Maghera NM & D 57   K6
Magherafelt M Ulst 61   Q4
Magheralin AB & C 56   E1
Magherally AB & C 56   F3
Magheramason D & S 66 B10
Magheramorne E Antr 63   L3
Magheraroarty/*Machaire*
Rabhartaigh Donegl 64   F6
Magheraveely/*Machaire*
Mhílic F & O 54   E7
Maghery AB & C 62 A10
Maghery/*Mhachaire*
Donegl 58   F1
Maguiresbridge F & O 54   B5
Mahoonagh Limrck 18   C8
Maigh Cuilinn/*Moycullen*
Galway 33   Q7
Maighros/*Moyrus* Galway .. 32   F7
Malahide/*Mullach Íde*
Dublin 39   N4
Malahide Castle &
Gardens Dublin 39   N4
Málainn Bhig/*Malin Beg*
Donegl 58   A6
Málainn Mhóir/*Malin*
More Donegl 58   B6
Malin/*Málainn* Donegl 66   D2
Malin Beg/*Málainn Bhig*
Donegl 58   A6
Malin Head Donegl 66   B1
Malin More/*Málainn*
Mhóir Donegl 58   B6
Mallow/*Mala* Cork 11   P5
Manorcunningham/
Mainéar Uí
Chuinneagáin Donegl ... 65 N10
Manorhamilton/*Cluainín*
Leitrm 52   G5
Manor Stone Services
Laois 29   J9
Mansfieldstown Louth 47   K4
Manulla Mayo 42   B6
Marble Arch Caves F & O .. 53   M6
Markethill AB & C 55   Q5
Marlfield Tippry 20 F10
Marshalstown Wexfd 22   H5
Martinstown E Antr 68 C10
Maulatrahane Cross
Roads Cork 4   F7
Mayglass Wexfd 15   N6
Maynooth/*Maigh Nuad*
Kildre 38   G6
Mayo Abbey Mayo 42   C8
Mayobridge NM & D 56   F7
Mazetown L & C 62 G10
McCormack's Cross Laois .. 29   M7
McElroystown E Antr 62   G1
McNead's Bridge Wmeath .. 37   N4
Meanus Limrck 18   H6
Meelick Clare 18   H2
Meenacarn/*Mín an*
Chairn Donegl 58   G2
Meenanare Kerry 17   J9
Meenscovane Kerry 17 K10
Meigh NM & D 56   D8
Melview Longfd 44   F8
Menlough/*Mionlach*
Galway 35   J5

Mhachaire/*Maghery*
Donegl 58   F1
Middletown AB & C 55   L5
Midleton/*Mainister na*
Corann Cork 6   G4
Milestone Tippry 19   Q3
Milford AB & C 55   N4
Milford/*Áth an Mhuilinn*
Cork 18 E10
Milford/*Baile na*
nGallóglach Donegl 65   M7
Millbrook E Antr 63   K2
Millbrook Meath 45   P8
Milleen Bridge Cork 4   F7
Milleens Cork 3   J5
Millisle A & ND 63   P7
Millstreet Cork 12   E3
Millstreet Watfd 12   L4
Millstreet/*Sráid an*
Mhuilinn Cork 10   H6
Milltown AB & C 55   M2
Milltown Cavan 54 B10
Milltown Dublin 39   J7
Milltown Galway 34   E1
Milltown Kildre 38 D10
Milltown L & C 62   H9
Milltown/*Baile an*
Mhuilinn Kerry 8   E4
Milltown/*Baile an*
Mhuilinn Kerry 9   N4
Milltown Malbay/*Sráid na*
Cathrach Clare 24   G9
Mín an Chairn/*Meenacarn*
Donegl 58   G2
Minane Bridge Cork 6   D7
Mitchelstown/*Baile*
Mhistéala Cork 12   D2
Mitchelstown Cave Tippry ... 12   F1
Moate/*An Móta* Wmeath .. 36   F6
Modelligo Watfd 13   L5
Model Village Cork 11   M9
Mogeely Cork 7   J3
Mohill/*Maothail* Leitrm ... 44   E4
Moira L & C 62 E10
Monagear/*Móin na gCaor*
Wexfd 23   J6
Monaghan/*Muineachán*
Monhan 55   J6
Monamolin Wexfd 23   L5
Monard Tippry 19   N7
Monaseed Wexfd 23   K2
Monaster Limrck 18   G6
Monasteraden Sligo 43   L4
Monasterevin/*Mainistir*
Eimhín Kildre 29   P2
Monavea Cross Laois 29   P9
Monea F & O 53   N2
Moneygall/*Muine Gall*
Offaly 27   P8
Moneygall Services
Tippry 27   P8
Moneyglass A & N 62   C4
Moneymore M Ulst 61   Q6
Moneyneany M Ulst 61   M3
Moneyreagh L & C 63   L9
Moneyslane AB & C 56   G5
Monivea/*Muine Mheá*
Galway 34   G6
Monkstown Cork 6   E5
Monmore Clare 16   H3
Montpelier Limrck 19   K1
Mooncoin/*Móin Choinn*
Kilken 14   C5
Mooney's Cross Laois 29   P8
Moore's Cross Laois 29   P9
Moorfields E Antr 62   F3
Mornington Meath 47   M8
Moss-Side CC & G 67   Q5
Mountain Barracks/*Red*
Hill Cork 12   E3
Mountbellew/*An Creagán*
Galway 35   K4
Mountbolus Offaly 28   F1
Mountcharles/*Moin*
Séarlas Donegl 59   J7
Mountfield F & O 60   H7
Mountjoy Cork 60   F7
Mountjoy M Ulst 61   R9
Mountmellick/*Móinteach*
Mílic Laois 29   L3
Mount Nugent Cavan 45   N6
Mountrath/*Maighean*
Rátha Laois 29   J6
Mount Rivers Watfd 13   K5
Mountshannon/*Baile Uí*
Bheoláin Clare 26   H7
Mount Stewart House &
Gardens A & ND 63   P9
Mount Talbot Roscom 35   N3

Mount Uniacke Cork 7   J2
Mount Usher Gardens
Wicklw 31   P5
Mourne Mountains
NM & D 56   H8
Moville/*Bun an Phobail*
Donegl 66   G5
Moy Galway 25   N3
Moy M Ulst 55   M1
Moycullen/*Maigh Cuilinn*
Galway 33   Q7
Moydow Longfd 44 F10
Moygashel M Ulst 61 P10
Moyglare Meath 38   G6
Moyglass Galway 26   G4
Moylough Galway 35   J4
Moylough Sligo 42   H2
Moyna Mayo 41   L6
Moynalty Meath 46   D7
Moyne Tippry 20   F2
Moyrhee Clare 25   N6
Moyrus/*Maighros* Galway .. 32   F7
Moyvally Kildre 38   C5
Moyvane/*Maigh Mheáin*
Kerry 17   K7
Moyvore Wmeath 36   H3
Muckalee Kilken 21   P1
Mucklagh Offaly 37   J9
Mucklagh Bridge Wicklw .. 31   K7
Muckross House Kerry 10   B7
Muff/*Magh* Donegl 66   D8
Mulhuddart Services
Dublin 39   K5
Mullagh Galway 35 L10
Mullagh Meath 38   G4
Mullagh/*An Mullach*
Cavan 46   C6
Mullagh/*Mullach* Clare .. 24 F10
Mullaghbane NM & D 56   B9
Mullaghmore/*An Mullach*
Mór Sligo 52   D1
Mullan's Corner AB & C ... 56   F2
Mullinacuft Wicklw 30 H10
Mullinahone/*Muileann*
na hUamhan Tippry 21   J6
Mullinalaghta Longfd 45   K6
Mullinavat/*Muileann an*
Bhata Kilken 14   D4
Mullingar/*An Muileann*
gCearr Wmeath 37   L3
Mullyleggan Bridge
AB & C 55   M2
Mulranny Mayo 40   H4
Multyfarnham/*Muilte*
Farannáin Wmeath 37   L1
Mungret/*Mungairit*
Limrck 18   G4
Munterconnacht Cavan 46   B7
Murrintown Wexfd 15   N5
Murrisk/*Muraisc* Mayo 41   K7
Murroe Limrck 19   L3
Myshall/*Míseal* Carlow 22   E2

N

Naas/*An Nás* Kildre 38 F10
Na Dúnaibh/*Downings*
Donegl 65   K5
Na Forbacha/*Furbogh*
Galway 33   P9
Naran Donegl 58   F3
Narraghmore/*An*
Fhorrach Mhór Kildre 30   D4
National Aquatic Centre
& AquaZone
Dublin 39   K6
National Sea Life Centre
Wicklw 39 P10
Naul Dublin 39   L1
Navan/*An Uaimh* Meath .. 46 G10
Neale Mayo 33   P2
Nenagh/*An tAonach*
Tippry 27   L9
Newbawn Wexfd 15   J4
Newbliss/*Cúil Darach*
Monhan 54   G8
Newbridge Limrck 18   C5
Newbridge/*Droichead*
Nua Galway 35   L3
Newbridge/*Droichead*
Nua Kildre 30   E1
Newbuildings D & S 66 C10
Newcastle Galway 34   G7
Newcastle NM & D 57   K6
Newcastle Tippry 13   K2
Newcastle/*An Caisleán*
Nua Dublin 38   H8

Newcastle/*An Caisleán Nua* Wicklw ... 31 P4
Newcastle West/*An Caisleán Nua* Limrck ... 17 P8
New Garden Limrck ... 19 K2
Newgrange Meath ... 47 K9
New Inn Galway ... 35 K8
New Inn/*Loch Ceann* Tippry ... 20 D8
Newmarket Kilken ... 21 N7
Newmarket/*Áth Trasna* Cork ... 11 J3
Newmarket on Fergus/*Cora Chaitlín* Clare ... 18 D1
Newmills Cork ... 5 J7
Newmills Donegl ... 59 P1
Newmills M Ulst ... 61 P9
Newport/*An Port Nua* Tippry ... 19 L2
Newport/*Baile Uí Fhiacháin* Mayo ... 41 L5
New Ross/*Ros Mhic Thriúin* Wexfd ... 14 G3
Newry NM & D ... 56 D7
Newtown Dublin ... 39 M9
Newtown Galway ... 34 E7
Newtown Galway ... 35 K4
Newtown Kildre ... 30 C2
Newtown Kildre ... 30 E3
Newtown Kildre ... 30 G2
Newtown Kildre ... 38 E6
Newtown Kildre ... 38 H7
Newtown Laois ... 29 N9
Newtown Meath ... 46 H6
Newtown Offaly ... 28 C1
Newtown Offaly ... 36 C9
Newtown Offaly ... 36 G6
Newtown Roscom ... 44 C7
Newtown Sligo ... 51 P3
Newtown Tippry ... 27 K8
Newtown Watfd ... 13 R3
Newtown Wexfd ... 14 F5
Newtown Wexfd ... 15 J7
Newtownabbey A & N ... 63 J6
Newtownards A & ND ... 63 M8
Newtownbutler F & O ... 54 D7
Newtowncashel Longfd ... 36 C2
Newtown Crommelin E Antr ... 68 C9
Newtowncunningham/*An Baile Nua* Donegl ... 65 Q9
Newtownforbes/*An Lios Breac* Longfd ... 44 F8
Newtownhamilton NM & D ... 55 P7
Newtownmountkennedy/*Baile an Chinnéidigh* Wicklw ... 31 P3
Newtownstewart D & S ... 60 F5
New Twopothouse Cork ... 11 N4
Nicker Limrck ... 19 M5
Ninemilehouse Tippry ... 21 K8
Nobber/*An Obair* Meath ... 46 F6
Nohoval Cork ... 6 D8
Nurney Kildre ... 30 C3
Nursetown More Cork ... 11 N6

O

O'Briensbridge/*Droichead Uí Bhriain* Clare ... 19 K1
O'Callaghansmills Clare ... 26 D9
Ogonnelloe Clare ... 26 G8
Oileáin Árann/*Aran Islands* Galway ... 24 B3
Oileán Chléire/*Cape Clear Island* Cork ... 4 B10
Oilgate/*Maolán na nGabhar* Wexfd ... 22 H8
Old Bushmills Distillery CC & G ... 67 N4
Oldcastle/*An Seanchaisleán* Meath ... 45 Q7
Old Jameson Distillery C Dubl ... 39 L7
Old Kilcullen Kildre ... 30 E3
Old Kilmeadan Watfd ... 14 C6
Old Leighlin Carlow ... 22 B1
Old Mill E Antr ... 63 K1
Old Pallas Limrck ... 19 M6
Old Pound Laois ... 29 N3
Old Ross Wexfd ... 14 H3
Oldtown Dublin ... 39 L3
Oldtown Roscom ... 36 C6
Omagh F & O ... 60 G8
Omeath/*Ó Méith* Louth ... 56 E9
Oola/*Úlla* Limrck ... 19 N6

Oram Monhan ... 55 N8
Oranmore/*Órán Mór* Galway ... 34 D9
Oristown/*Baile Órthaí* Meath ... 46 E8
Oughterard/*Uachtar Ard* Galway ... 33 N5
Oulart/*An tAbhallort* Wexfd ... 23 K6
Our Lady's Island Wexfd ... 15 Q7
Ovens Cork ... 11 N10
Owenahincha Cork ... 5 J7
Owning Kilken ... 21 L9

P

Palatine Carlow ... 30 D9
Pallas Cork ... 3 L3
Pallas Green Limrck ... 19 M5
Pallaskenry Limrck ... 18 E3
Palmerstown Dublin ... 39 K7
Park D & S ... 61 J2
Parke Mayo ... 42 B4
Parkgate A & N ... 62 G5
Parteen Clare ... 18 H2
Partry Mayo ... 41 Q9
Passage East/*An Pasáiste* Watfd ... 14 G6
Passage West/*An Pasáiste* Cork ... 6 E5
Patrickswell/*Tobar Phádraig* Limrck ... 18 G5
Paulstown/*Baile Phóil* Kilken ... 22 B3
Paulstown Services Kilken ... 22 B3
Pettigo/*Paiteagó* Donegl ... 59 P9
Phelim's Cross Laois ... 29 N7
Philipstown Louth ... 47 K6
Piercetown Cork ... 6 C7
Piercetown Wexfd ... 15 N5
Piltown/*Baile an Phoill* Kilken ... 21 M10
Piperstown Louth ... 47 L7
Plumbridge D & S ... 60 G4
Poles Cavan ... 45 N3
Pollagh Mayo ... 40 D3
Pollagh Offaly ... 36 F8
Poll an tSomais/*Pollatomish* Mayo ... 48 H4
Pollardstown Cork ... 12 D2
Pollatomish/*Poll an tSomais* Mayo ... 48 H4
Pomeroy M Ulst ... 61 L8
Pontoon Mayo ... 42 B3
Portadown AB & C ... 56 C2
Portaferry A & ND ... 57 P2
Portahack Donegl ... 66 E2
Portarlington/*Cúil an tSúdaire* Laois ... 29 M2
Portavogie A & ND ... 57 R1
Portballintrae CC & G ... 67 N4
Portbradden CC & G ... 67 Q4
Portglenone E Antr ... 62 B2
Port Laoise/*Portlaoise* Laois ... 29 L5
Portlaw/*Port Lách* Watfd ... 14 B5
Portmagee/*An Caladh* Kerry ... 8 D10
Portmarnock/*Port Mearnóg* Dublin ... 39 N5
Portnablagh/*Port na Bláiche* Donegl ... 65 J5
Portnakilly Mayo ... 40 E7
Portnoo Donegl ... 58 E3
Portrane Dublin ... 39 P3
Portroe/*An Port Rua* Tippry ... 27 J8
Portrush CC & G ... 67 M4
Portsalon/*Port an tSalainn* Donegl ... 65 N4
Portstewart CC & G ... 67 L5
Portumna/*Port Omna* Galway ... 27 L4
Poulnamucky Tippry ... 20 E9
Powerscourt House & Gardens Wicklw ... 31 N1
Poyntzpass AB & C ... 56 D5
Prehen D & S ... 66 C9
Prosperous/*An Chorrchoill* Kildre ... 38 E8
Puckaun/*Pocán* Tippry ... 27 K7
Pullincha Cork ... 3 K5

Q

Quakers Cross Roads Cork ... 4 H7
Quay Village Mayo ... 50 G7

Quigley's Point Donegl ... 66 E6
Quilty Clare ... 24 F10
Quin/*Cuinche* Clare ... 25 P10
Quitrent Cork ... 12 A2

R

Raghly Sligo ... 51 N3
Raghrabeg Roscom ... 35 Q8
Rahan Offaly ... 36 H8
Rahara Roscom ... 35 Q3
Raharney/*Ráth Fhearna* Wmeath ... 37 P3
Raheen Laois ... 29 K6
Raheen Wexfd ... 15 J3
Raheen Cross Roads Cork ... 4 F8
Raheny C Dubl ... 39 N6
Raholp NM & D ... 57 N3
Ráith/*Ray* Donegl ... 64 H6
Raloo E Antr ... 63 K3
Ramelton/*Ráth Mealtain* Donegl ... 65 N8
Ramoy Monhan ... 54 G6
Ramsgrange Wexfd ... 14 G6
Randalstown A & N ... 62 D4
Raphoe/*Ráth Bhoth* Donegl ... 60 C2
Rasharkin CC & G ... 67 P10
Rathangan/*Ráth Iomgháin* Kildre ... 38 B10
Rathbeggan Meath ... 38 H4
Rathcarran/*Ráth Chairn* Meath ... 38 D1
Ráth Chairn/*Rathcarran* Meath ... 38 D1
Rathcoole/*Ráth Cúil* Dublin ... 39 J8
Rathcormac/*Ráth Chormaic* Cork ... 12 D6
Rathdangan Wicklw ... 30 H7
Rathdowney/*Ráth Domhnaigh* Laois ... 28 G9
Rathdrum/*Ráth Droma* Wicklw ... 31 M7
Rathfarnham Dublin ... 39 L8
Ráth Fhearna/*Raharney* Wmeath ... 37 P3
Rathfriland AB & C ... 56 F6
Rathgarogue Wexfd ... 22 D8
Rathgormuck Watfd ... 13 P1
Rathkeale/*Ráth Caola* Limrck ... 18 D6
Rathlin Island CC & G ... 68 C2
Rathmave Meath ... 38 G2
Rathmolyon Meath ... 38 D4
Rathmore/*An Ráth Mhór* Kerry ... 10 F6
Rathmore/*An Ráth Mhór* Kildre ... 38 H10
Rathmullan/*Ráth Maoláin* Donegl ... 65 P7
Rathnew/*Ráth Naoi* Wicklw ... 31 P5
Rathnure Wexfd ... 22 E7
Rathowen/*Ráth Eoghain* Wmeath ... 45 K10
Rathvilly/*Ráth Bhile* Carlow ... 30 F8
Rathwire Wmeath ... 37 P3
Ratoath/*Ráth Tó* Meath ... 39 J3
Ravernet L & C ... 62 H10
Ray/*Ráith* Donegl ... 64 H6
Recess/*Sraith Salach* Galway ... 32 H4
Redcastle Donegl ... 66 F5
Redcross/*An Chrois Dhearg* Wicklw ... 31 N8
Redhills/*An Cnoc Rua* Cavan ... 54 D9
Redmonds Bridge Wicklw ... 30 G7
Reen Cork ... 3 M5
Reenascreena Cork ... 4 H6
Reenroe Cork ... 2 H5
Rerrin Cork ... 3 L6
Rhode/*Ród* Offaly ... 37 N7
Richhill AB & C ... 55 P3
Ringaskiddy/*Rinn an Scidigh* Cork ... 6 E6
Ringville Kilken ... 14 F5
Ringville/*An Rinn* Watfd ... 13 N7
Riverchapel Wexfd ... 23 M3
Riverstick Cork ... 6 C7
Riverstown Cork ... 6 D3
Riverstown Offaly ... 28 C4
Riverstown/*Baile idir dhá Abhainn* Sligo ... 52 D8
Robeen Mayo ... 42 B9
Roberts Cove Cork ... 6 E8

Robertstown/*Baile Riobaird* Kildre ... 38 D8
Robinstown Meath ... 38 E1
Rochfortbridge Wmeath ... 37 M5
Rockcorry/*Buíochar* Monhan ... 54 H9
Rock of Cashel Tippry ... 20 D6
Rolestown Dublin ... 39 L3
Roonah Quay Mayo ... 40 F7
Roosky/*Rúscaigh* Roscom ... 44 D6
Rosahane Bridge Wicklw ... 31 K8
Ros an Mhíl/*Rossaveel* Galway ... 33 K8
Rosbercon Wexfd ... 14 G3
Roscam C Gal ... 34 D8
Roscommon/*Ros Comáin* Roscom ... 35 P1
Roscrea/*Ros Cré* Tippry ... 28 D7
Rosegreen Tippry ... 20 E7
Rosenallis Laois ... 29 J3
Roskelton Cross Laois ... 29 J6
Ross Mayo ... 41 Q4
Rossaveel/*Ros an Mhíl* Galway ... 33 K8
Rossbaun Laois ... 28 F6
Ross Behy Kerry ... 9 J6
Rosscahill Galway ... 33 P6
Rosscarbery/*Ros Ó gCairbre* Cork ... 4 H7
Ross Castle Kerry ... 9 Q7
Rossdorragha Laois ... 28 F6
Rossduff Watfd ... 14 F7
Rosses Point/*An Ros* Sligo ... 51 P4
Rossinver Leitrm ... 52 H3
Rosslare/*Ros Láir* Wexfd ... 15 Q6
Rosslare Harbour Wexfd ... 15 Q6
Rosslea F & O ... 54 F6
Rossnowlagh Donegl ... 59 J9
Rostrevor NM & D ... 56 F9
Roundstone/*Cloch na Rón* Galway ... 32 E5
Roundwood/*An Tóchar* Wicklw ... 31 M4
Rousky F & O ... 60 H5
Ruan Clare ... 25 M7
Rush/*An Ros* Dublin ... 39 P3
Rushin Cross Laois ... 28 H5
Russborough House & Parklands Wicklw ... 30 H2
Ryefield Cavan ... 46 B7
Rylane Kerry ... 17 K9
Rylane Cross Cork ... 11 L8

S

Saggart/*Teach Sagard* Dublin ... 39 J8
Saintfield NM & D ... 57 L1
St Johnston/*Baile Suingean* Donegl ... 60 D1
St Margaret's Dublin ... 39 L5
St Mullins Carlow ... 22 C7
St Patrick's Cathedral C Dubl ... 39 M7
Saleen Cork ... 6 G5
Sallins/*Na Solláin* Kildre ... 38 F9
Sallybrook Cork ... 6 D3
Salthill C Gal ... 34 B9
Saltmills Wexfd ... 14 H7
Sandholes M Ulst ... 61 N8
Sandpit Louth ... 47 M7
Santry C Dubl ... 39 M6
Saul NM & D ... 57 N3
Scarriff/*An Scairbh* Clare ... 26 F8
Scartaglin/*Scairteach an Ghlinne* Kerry ... 10 C4
Scarva AB & C ... 56 D4
Sceilg Mhichíl/*Skellig Michael* Kerry ... 2 A2
School Cross Laois ... 28 F9
Schull/*An Scoil* Cork ... 3 Q8
Science Gallery C Dubl ... 39 M7
Scotch Street AB & C ... 55 Q1
Scotshouse Monhan ... 54 F9
Scotstown/*Baile an Scotaigh* Monhan ... 54 H5
Scrahanagaur Kerry ... 3 K1
Scramoge Roscom ... 44 C8
Screen Wexfd ... 23 K8
Seaforde NM & D ... 57 L4
Seapoint Louth ... 47 N7
Semple Stadium Tippry ... 20 E3
Seskinore F & O ... 60 G10
Shanagarry Cork ... 7 J5
Shanaglish Galway ... 25 P5
Shanagolden/*Seanghualainn* Limrck ... 17 P5
Shanbally Cork ... 6 E6

Shanballymore/An
    Seanbhaile Mór Cork 11 R3
Shankill/Seanchill Dublin 39 P9
Shannon/Sionainn Clare...... 18 E2
Shannon Airport Clare........ 18 D2
Shannonbridge/
    Droichead na Sionainne
    Offaly 36 B8
Shannon Harbour Offaly..... 36 C10
Shannonvale Cork 5 K6
Sheffield Cross Laois.......... 29 L5
Shercock/Searcóg Cavan.... 46 D2
Sherkin Island Cork 4 C10
Shillelagh/Síol Éalaigh
    Wicklw............................. 22 H1
Shinrone/Suí an Róin
    Offaly 28 C6
Shrigley NM & D 57 N2
Shrule/Shruthair Mayo........ 34 B3
Silverbridge NM & D 55 Q9
Silvermines/Béal Átha
    Gabhann Tippry............... 27 K10
Simonstown Wmeath.......... 45 M9
Sion Mills D & S 60 D4
Sixmilebridge/Droichead
    Abhann Ó gCearnaigh
    Clare................................ 18 F1
Sixmilecross F & O............. 61 J9
Skeeheenarinky Tippry 12 F1
Skehanagh Galway............. 34 H5
Skeheen Mayo.................... 43 J4
Skellig Michael/Sceilg
    Mhichíl Kerry.................... 2   A2
Skerries/Na Sceirí Dublin.... 39 P1
Skerries Mills Dublin 39 P2
Skibbereen/An Sciobairín
    Cork 4   E8
Skreen Meath..................... 38 H1
Slade/An Slaod Wexfd 14 G9
Slane/Baile Shláine Meath .. 47 J9
Slane Castle Meath 46 H9
Slatta Roscom.................... 44 D7
Slieve Gullion Forest Park
    NM & D 56 C8
Slieve League Cliffs
    Donegl 58 B7
Slieverue Kilken 14 E6
Sligo/Sligeach Sligo........... 52 C5
Sligo Airport Sligo.............. 51 P4
Smithborough Monhan 54 G6
Sneem/An Snaidhm Kerry .. 3   K1
Snugborough Bridge
    Wicklw.............................. 30 H5
Somer Galway..................... 35 N9
Sooey Sligo........................ 52 D8
Spa Kerry 9   M1
Spa NM & D 57 K3
Spanish Point/Rinn na
    Spáinneach Clare............. 24 F9
Spaville Watfd..................... 20 G10
Spiddal/An Spidéal
    Galway.............................. 33 N9
Springfield F & O................ 53 N3
Srah Offaly......................... 36 F8
Srah/An tSraith Mayo......... 48 H2
Srahnamanragh Mayo......... 48 H9
Sraith Salach/Recess
    Galway.............................. 32 H4
Stabannan Louth 47 K5
Staplestown Kildre 38 E7
Stepaside/An Céime
    Dublin 39 M9
Stewartstown M Ulst........... 61 Q8
Stillorgan Dublin 39 N8
Stonehall Limrck 18 E4
Stonepark Donegl............... 59 J7
Stonepark Longfd............... 44 F9
Stoneyford Kilken 21 N6
Stoneyford L & C................ 62 G8
Strabane D & S 60 D3
Stradbally Kerry 8   H2
Stradbally/An Sráidbhaile
    Laois................................ 29 N5
Stradbally/An
    tSráidbhaile Watfd 13 Q5
Stradone/Sraith an
    Domhain Cavan 45 P3
Straffan Kildre 38 G2
Straid A & N. 63 J4
Strandhill/An Leathros
    Sligo................................ 51 P4
Strangford NM & D 57 P3
Stranocum CC & G 67 Q6
Stranorlar/Srath an Urláir
    Donegl 59 P3
Stratford/Áth na Sráide
    Wicklw.............................. 30 F6
Streedagh Sligo.................. 51 P1
Street/Sraid Wmeath.......... 45 K9

Strokestown/Béal na
    mBuillí Roscom 44 B7
Strokestown Park &
    Famine Museum
    Roscom 44 B7
Stroove/An tSrúibh
    Donegl 66 H4
Stuake Cork 11 M8
Summerhill/Cnoc an
    Línsigh Meath.................. 38 E4
Suncroft Kildre 30 D3
Sutton Dublin 39 P6
Swan Laois.......................... 29 N8
Swanlinbar/An Muileann
    Iarainn Cavan................... 53 N7
Swatragh M Ulst................. 61 Q1
Swinford/Béal Átha na
    Muice Mayo...................... 42 E4
Swords/Sord Dublin 39 M4

T

Tacumshane Wexfd 15 P7
Taghmon/Teach Munna
    Wexfd 15 L5
Tagoat Wexfd...................... 15 P6
Tallaght/Tamhlacht Dublin .. 39 K8
Tallanstown Louth 47 J4
Tallow/Tulach an Iarainn
    Watfd................................ 12 G6
Tallowbridge Watfd 12 G6
Tamlaght F & O................... 53 Q4
Tamlaght M Ulst................. 61 R1
Tandragee AB & C 56 C3
Tankardstown Cork............. 12 A2
Tara Meath.......................... 38 G2
Tarbert/Tairbeart Kerry 17 K5
Tashinny Longfd.................. 36 F1
Taugheen Mayo................... 42 C9
Taylorstown E Antr.............. 62 C3
Taylorstown Roscom........... 36 C6
Tayto Park Meath................ 39 J2
Tealane Cross Laois........... 29 K7
Teelin/Teileann Donegl........ 58 C7
Teemore F & O 54 B8
Teileann/Teelin Donegl........ 58 C7
Temple L & C...................... 63 K10
Templeglantine Limrck 17 N9
Templemore/An Teampall
    Mór Tippry........................ 28 D10
Templenoe Kerry................. 3   N1
Templepatrick A & N 62 G5
Templepatrick Services
    A & N 62 H6
Templeshanbo Wexfd 22 F5
Templetouhy/Teampall
    Tuaithe Tippry 28 E10
Tempo F & O 54 C3
Termon/An Tearmann
    Donegl 65 L8
Termonbarry/Tearmann
    Bearaigh Longfd 44 E8
Termonfeckin/Tearmann
    Feichín Louth................... 47 M7
Terryglass Tippry 27 L4
Tervoe Limrck 18 G3
The Burren Clare 25 K4
The Bush Louth 47 N2
The Butts Carlow 21 Q1
The Harrow/An Bráca
    Wexfd 23 K5
The Loup M Ulst................. 61 R6
The Model Sligo 52 C5
The Rock M Ulst................. 61 N8
Thomastown Kildre 38 E9
Thomastown Meath............ 45 Q9
Thomastown Tippry 20 B7
Thomastown/Baile Mhic
    Andáin Kilken................... 21 P6
Three Bridges Wicklw......... 30 G7
Thurles/Durlas Tippry 20 E3
Tiknock Wicklw 31 N10
Timahoe/Tigh Mochua
    Laois................................ 29 M6
Timoleague/Tigh Molaige
    Cork 5   M6
Tinahely/Tigh na hÉille
    Wicklw.............................. 31 J10
Tinryland Carlow 30 C10
Tinure Louth 47 K7
Tipperary/Tiobraid Árann
    Tippry............................... 19 P7
Tipperkevin Kildre 30 G2
Titanic Belfast Belfst.......... 63 K7
Tobercurry/Tubbercurry/
    Tobar an Choire Sligo....... 42 H1
Tobergregan Dublin 39 K2
Tobermore M Ulst............... 61 P3

Togher Cross Laois 29 J7
Tóin an tSeanbhaile/
    Tonatanvally Mayo 40 F2
Tombrack Wexfd.................. 22 H4
Tomhaggard/Teach
    Moshagard Wexfd 15 N7
Tonatanvally/Tóin an
    tSeanbhaile Mayo............ 40 F2
Toome A & N....................... 62 B4
Toomevara/Tuaim Uí
    Mheára Tippry.................. 27 N9
Tooraneena Watfd 13 L3
Tooreen Mayo..................... 42 G6
Toormore Cork 3   P8
Toraigh/Tory Island
    Donegl 64 F3
Tory Island/Toraigh
    Donegl 64 F3
Tourin Watfd 13 J5
Tourmakeady/Tuar Mhic
    Éadaigh Mayo.................. 41 N10
Tower Cork.......................... 11 P10
Townacurra Galway............ 32 E1
Tracashel Cork 3   Q4
Tragumna Cork 4   E9
Tralee/Trá Lí Kerry.............. 9   N2
Tramore/Trá Mhór Watfd..... 14 D8
Trillick F & O...................... 54 B1
Trim/Baile Átha Troim
    Meath 38 E2
Trim Castle Meath 38 E2
Trineens Cork..................... 5   L7
Tuam/Tuaim Galway........... 34 E3
Tuamgraney Clare 26 F8
Tuar Mhic Éadaigh/
    Tourmakeady Mayo.......... 41 N10
Tubbercurry/Tobercurry/
    Tobar an Choire Sligo....... 42 H1
Tubbrid Tippry 12 H1
Tubride Meath..................... 45 P8
Tulla/An Tulach Clare 26 C9
Tullaghan/An Tulachán
    Leitrm 52 E1
Tullamore/Tulach Mhór
    Offaly 37 J8
Tullaroan/Tullach Ruain
    Kilken 21 K3
Tullow/An Tulach Carlow..... 30 F10
Tully Galway........................ 32 D1
Tullyallen Louth 47 K8
Tullycreevy F & O............... 53 N3
Tully Cross Galway............. 32 E1
Tullyderrin Leitrm 53 J3
Tullyhommon F & O............ 59 P9
Tullynacross L & C............. 62 H9
Tullyvin Cavan.................... 45 Q1
Tulsk/Tuilsce Roscom......... 43 P7
Turlough Clare 25 L3
Turlough/Turlach Mayo....... 42 B5
Turlough Park & Museum
    of Country Life Mayo 42 B5
Turris Hill Donegl................ 59 J7
Tweedmount Cork............... 6   B3
Twomileborris Tippry 20 F3
Two Mile House Kildre 30 F2
Tylagh Kerry 9   Q1
Tynagh/Tine Galway........... 26 H2
Tynan AB & C...................... 55 L4
Tyrrellspass/Bealach an
    Tirialaigh Wmeath............ 37 L6
Tyrrelstown Dublin 39 K5

U

Ulster American Folk
    Park F & O 60 F7
Ulster Museum Belfst.......... 63 J8
Upper Ballinderry L & C 62 F9
Upperchurch Tippry............ 20 B2
Upperlands M Ulst.............. 61 Q1
Upton Cork.......................... 5   N3
Urlaur Mayo........................ 42 H6
Urlingford/Áth na
    nUrlainn Kilken................ 20 H2

V

Valentia Island Kerry.......... 8   D9
Valleymount Wicklw............ 30 H3
Ventry/Ceann Trá Kerry...... 8   D4
Ventry/Fionntrá Kerry.......... 8   D4
Vicarstown/Baile an
    Bhiocáire Laois................ 29 P4
Victoria Bridge D & S......... 60 E4
Villierstown/An Baile Nua
    Watfd................................ 13 K6

Virginia/Achadh an Iúir
    Cavan............................... 46 B6

W

Walshisland Offaly.............. 37 N9
Ward Cross Dublin.............. 39 L4
Waringstown AB & C........... 56 E1
Warrenpoint NM & D........... 56 E9
Watch House Village
    Wexfd 22 G2
Waterdyke Cork 11 R3
Waterfall Cork 5   Q1
Waterfoot CC & G............... 68 E7
Waterford/Port Láirge
    Watfd................................ 14 E6
Waterford Airport Watfd...... 14 E8
Watergrasshill/Cnocán
    na Biolraí Cork 12 C8
Waterville/An Coireán
    Kerry................................ 2   G1
Weir Village Galway............ 34 E10
Wellingtonbridge/
    Droichead Eoin Wexfd...... 15 K6
Westport/Cathair na Mart
    Mayo................................ 41 L7
Westport House Mayo 41 L7
Wexford/Loch Garman
    Wexfd 15 N4
Whitechurch Cork 6   B2
Whitechurch Watfd 13 L5
Whitechurch Wexfd 14 G5
Whitecross NM & D 56 B6
Whitegate/An Geata Bán
    Clare................................ 27 J7
Whitegate/An Geata Bán
    Cork 6   F6
Whitehall Roscom............... 44 E8
Whitehall Bridge Galway..... 35 P8
Whitehead E Antr 63 M4
Wicklow/Cill Mhantáin
    Wicklw.............................. 31 Q6
Wicklow Mountains
    National Park Wicklw........ 31 K3
Wicklow Services Wicklw.... 31 P4
Williamstown Galway 43 K10
Willville Louth 47 P2
Windgap/Bearna na
    Gaoithe Kilken 21 L8
Woodenbridge Wicklw......... 31 M9
Woodford/An Ghráig
    Galway.............................. 26 H4
Woodlawn Galway............... 35 K7
Woodstock Gardens &
    Arboretum Kilken 21 Q7
Wright's Cross Kildre 30 B6

Y

Youghal Tippry 27 J8
Youghal/Eochaill Cork 7   M3

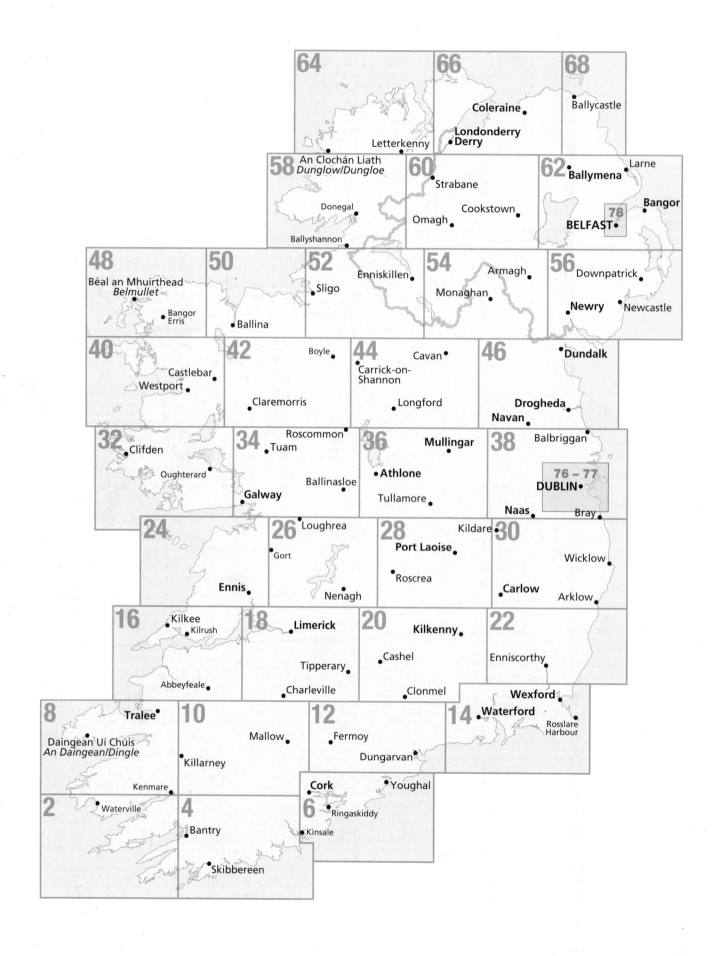

64	66 Coleraine	68 Ballycastle

Londonderry
Derry
Letterkenny

58 An Clochán Liath
Dunglow/Dungloe
Donegal
Ballyshannon

60
Strabane
Cookstown
Omagh

62 Ballymena
Larne
Bangor
BELFAST 78

48 Béal an Mhuirthead
Belmullet
Bangor Erris

50
Ballina

52 Sligo
Enniskillen

54
Armagh
Monaghan

56 Downpatrick
Newry
Newcastle

40 Castlebar
Westport

42
Boyle
Claremorris

44 Cavan
Carrick-on-Shannon
Longford

46 Dundalk
Drogheda
Navan

32 Clifden
Oughterard

34 Roscommon
Tuam
Ballinasloe
Galway

36 Mullingar
Athlone
Tullamore

38 Balbriggan
76 – 77
DUBLIN
Naas
Bray

24

26 Loughrea
Gort
Ennis
Nenagh

28 Kildare
Port Laoise
Roscrea

30
Wicklow
Carlow
Arklow

16 Kilkee
Kilrush

18 Limerick
Tipperary
Charleville
Abbeyfeale

20 Kilkenny
Cashel
Clonmel

22
Enniscorthy
Wexford
Waterford
Rosslare Harbour

8 Tralee
Daingean Uí Chúis
An Daingean/Dingle
Kenmare

10
Mallow
Killarney

12 Fermoy
Dungarvan

14

2 Waterville

4 Bantry
Skibbereen

6 Cork
Youghal
Ringaskiddy
Kinsale

0	10	20	30	40	50 miles
0	20	40	60		80 km